Others

Others

BLAINE M. YORGASON

and

BRENTON G. YORGASON

Bookcraft
Salt Lake City, Utah

Library of Congress Catalog Card Number: 78-67218
ISBN O-88494-349-6

9th Printing, 1981

Lithographed in the United States of America
PUBLISHERS PRESS
Salt Lake City, Utah

This book is affectionately dedicated to
our very special families:

Kathy, Tami, Nate, Steve
Travis, Danny, Michelle

Margaret, Jason, Aaron
Jeremy, Joshua, Jennifer

The Gift

The gasp
from the crowd was
audible
And a few smiles even
vanished
As the mallet drove the first
spike
Through the torn
and bleeding
hand.

With haste and little care
the other monstrous
nails
Were blasted through
His flesh
And He was lifted, silent, naked,
blood-covered and agonizing
Amid the jeers, the applause, the lust
of the ones He loved
so dearly.

Dark clouds boiled, winds tore
at the rocky summit
As the people slapped and mocked
and spit
And taught their children—
Yet in silence He endured, weeping
not in pain but pity
For these He loved
had
still
so awfully far to go.

Eyes closed, He
spoke often
with His Father, who stood
very near, of Gethsemane
and the torment which left His blood
to stain the ground
Atoning for this so great
a sin
And all others, past and
yet to come.

Anguish-filled hours dragged
slowly by
As He hung trembling because
of pain
And suffering
both body and spirit
Till the Father in perfect
love
and understanding
Withdrew.

Now alone and
totally so
The Son cried out
in agony of
spirit,
Shrinking—
MY GOD
MY GOD
Why hast thou
forsaken me?

And then a time
Only moments perhaps
But longer than all
Eternity
When the Son, lonely still
and in silence
Partook of the bitter cup
And finished His sacrifice
for the children
of men.

Father, the glory be
Thine
I have given the gift
Thou sent me forth
to give—
My love for them is now perfect
that theirs may one day be.
It is finished!
Into Thy hands, as always
I commend
my spirit.

– *Blaine M. Yorgason*

CONTENTS

ACKNOWLEDGMENTS

Appreciation is sincerely tendered to all those whose contributions have made this book possible. We are especially indebted to our parents, Gayle, Beatrice and Lucy Yorgason, whose timely example and constant love have enabled us to retain, as brothers, a special closeness and confidence in each other. To our wives, Kathy and Margaret, we express our eternal love. While Margaret helped with the children, Kathy spent endless hours in typing and in editing—and for their "caring" we give our thanks.

Many friends have given of themselves in sharing personal experiences and testimonies. While some wished to remain unidentified, they, as well as those whose names appear below, know of our gratitude.

Finally, and most importantly, we are eternally indebted to our Savior, Jesus Christ, who taught us to care both by precept and example.

CONTRIBUTORS

Tom Adams
Dee Anne Chandler
Chris Davis
Linda Lee
Ronda Kunzler
Cathy Larson
Galen Chock
Kevin Imlay
Tracy Erickson
Reggie Sellers

Brad Egan
Heather Tatom
Zina Walch
Scott Elkins
Rita Elkins
Kevin James O'day
Cindy Dew
Cindy Lowder
Gwen Schlessman
Shellie Rydalch

Joni Clements
Richard Murdock
Karen Ensign
Nancy Brown
Catherine Rodebach
Anne Visser
Phyllis Inouye
Renee Shout
LaNell Dye
Denae Godfrey
Linda Anderson
Ann Roberts
Pam Kincaid
Charlotte Monson
Mark Kastleman
Bill Waite
Ruth Burr
Kenneth Burr
Connie Johnson
Jacqueline Dennis

Russell Crump
Erin Riley
Amalea Wright
Brad Wright
Lisa Taylor
Kathy Russell
Carol Abbott
Pam Watson
Debbie Kausen
Mark Hendrickson
Craig Adams
Laurie Crookell
Edward Platt
Jeff Gustin
Suzie M. Beck
Kristi Jorgensen
Linda Furness
Dale Steiner
LaVar Thornock

1

FILLING UP, FLOWING OUT

❝ "Today my husband named and blessed our first child, a boy, and my heart was full of gratitude for my blessings and also full of gratitude and love for the group of girls who made possible this wonderful life I now have.

"I came from a family of four. My mother was LDS, but my father had no religious beliefs, However, he was intolerant toward the Mormon Church. There was great discord, many arguments, and much bitterness in our home. My parents quarreled constantly, both verbally and physically.

"We paid a price. At sixteen my older brother had been convicted on a narcotics charge and had been placed in a detention home. I was fourteen and headed down that same road.

"I had been baptized at eight and had always attended Sunday School with my mother. Now, at fourteen, I went to church only to get out of the house and keep peace with my mom.

"I'll never forget the first Sunday some girls from my Mutual class came around to invite me to Mutual. Four girls! Two of them were cheerleaders at Central Junior High where we all went to school. The other two girls I had, of course, seen at church and school and knew were popular and well liked.

"How I hated those girls! I hated them because they were everything I wanted to be and couldn't. I was nothing, I was low-class—I knew it and I knew they knew it, too. I hated them all. I took their crummy little invitation note and smugly lied that I'd be sure and make it out to Mutual. Of course, I never went.

"This story could have ended there. Those four girls had done their duty at the beginning of the year. I had been personally invited out to Mutual and had refused. What more could they do?

"Fortunately for me, the story did not end there. In the months that followed, every Sunday one of those four girls would be at my door with an invitation. But she wouldn't just drop it off and leave. Each girl would stay and talk to me for at least an hour. At first this was ridiculous. We would talk about the weather and about Sunday School, which were the only two things I had in common with them, and then we would sit through eternal silences.

"Gradually our conversations became closer. The girls always seemed so eager to listen to my ideas and problems. They never yelled at me or called me names. And yet I was still apprehensive and I still disliked them greatly. I never attended Mutual.

"After three months, my Mutual teacher called and offered to pick me up for Mutual. 'That will be fine,' I said, lying again, knowing I would now simply plan to be gone on Tuesday nights just to show them.

"And I was gone. I would go to my friends' houses—my real friends, where I belonged. Some people would think they were undesirable because of the things we did, but I thought they were great because they cared about me—or at least I thought they did.

"Time went on, yet those same four girls never gave up. They took a special interest in me. They always said 'hi' at school and would stop and talk to me. They sat by me in classes. They found out which subjects I was flunking (due mostly to lack of study) and would invite themselves over to study with me.

"I could not understand it. Why me? They knew the things I did—my reputation. Surely they felt my resentment toward them. Why did they keep on trying? I knew I was a lost cause. I felt pushed and cornered, my own conscience hurting. Still I fought them.

"December 12 was my birthday. Not a special day, really. My family never made birthdays special. I got a 'happy birthday' from my mom and nothing from my dad, and I went through the school day not letting anyone know I was a year older. I planned on celebrating that night by sneaking out and going over to see some friends.

"At 8:00 the doorbell rang. I answered it and there stood my Mutual class. One girl had a cake in her hands and another a gallon of ice cream. They were all smiling and suddenly broke out into 'Happy Birthday.' I didn't even know how to react.

"I went to Mutual twice that month and once in January. But that was all. It wasn't that I didn't want to go to Mutual. The three times I attended were great and I felt a strange closeness toward those four girls, but the social pressure from my other friends was too great and after leading the kind of life I led all week, I just couldn't face those Mutual girls. Still they befriended me and never judged.

"March 12 was a very dreary day in my life. I came home from school late. I had flunked an exam that afternoon and was very blue. I came home to find my parents in a very heated argument. Knowing how it would be, I went to my room and sat there, numb, just listening. I don't remember much after that except losing all control.

"You wonder why I add this event to my letter? Well, its significance didn't come until a few days later when I gained consciousness in the hospital. I found out I would be in there for about three weeks.

"For three weeks I lay in the hospital and for three weeks not one of my friends came to see me. Not one! The very friends I had always gotten kicks with. Where were they now when I needed their friendship?

"Instead, every day at 3:30 one of those four Mutual girls would be at my side. They were there every day. They brought me things to read, they sneaked in candy, and they brought in a transistor radio for me to listen to. We would do crossword puzzles together, and they would tell me the latest happenings at school. They never asked what happened and I never offered to tell.

"After I got out of the hospital I began to go to Mutual. I finally realized that those four girls who had taken an interest in me really were sincere. Not only had I grown to like them, but now I felt a bond of love between us. My life seemed to be going so much better. I was happier than I had ever been.

"April 2 was a day I shall never forget. It was a cold, dark, rainy day, a depressing day. During the final period of school, the principal walked into the room with a note for me. I was to go home immediately. 'What now?' was my only thought. I grabbed my books and sweater and ran out.

"It was pouring rain. I was glad I only lived four blocks from school, and yet with each block I felt a greater and greater despair. What was wrong at home?

"By the time I reached the house I knew something dreadful had happened. I raced through the front door and almost collided head-on with my dad. I looked up into a ghostly white tear-streaked face, a face I had never seen before. He was trembling all over and could only mutter, 'She's gone, your mother's passed away.'

"Oh, how I loved her! I was stunned. I turned and I began to

3

run. I ran and ran and my tears mixed with the rain. I ran until I was exhausted, but I did not stop. My face was swollen and my head hurt. Still I ran. Then, suddenly, I saw from the opposite direction someone coming toward me. I paused and wiped my eyes. Could it be? One of those four Mutual girls, the girls who truly cared about me. One of those girls was running through the rain for me. I began to run again and when we met I threw my arms around that girl and we both collapsed to the ground. I sat there crying, and she cried with me.

"In the years that followed, I became one with those four Mutual girls. I learned to care, really care about others and to give of myself. I found that by helping others my own problems diminished.

"When the most important day of my life came, I knelt across the altar from my sweetheart and in the reflection of mirrors were those four Mutual girls, standing, with tears running down their cheeks. They had made this possible for me.

"I'll never know why I had been so important to them. Me, a nobody. I can only thank my Father in heaven for those girls and pray with all my heart that there are many more like them in his Church." **"**

Where does love for others begin?

Some people, like the four Mutual girls, seem to be inwardly in tune to the needs of others. They *notice* when other people are in need. Most opportunities for service aren't really obvious, however. Frequently the opportunity to care is hidden and can best be discovered in the weary or the sad, the grief-stricken or the lonely. To make caring and service even more difficult, the needy person's natural pride frequently forces him to hide his need from the very people who are best able to help.

How can those secret and yet vitally important needs be discovered? It isn't as hard as it sometimes seems. But to see people's needs, you have to be *looking.* You have to be curious about other people.

Curious? Doesn't that mean prying into other people's secrets?

Well, in a sense, it does. But there are many motives for curiosity. A gossip learns all he can about his neighbors in order to poison their reputations so he can enhance his own. Some morbid people are curious about other people's disasters because, for some reason, disaster adds some excitement to their lives. Others are only curious about famous people, or beautiful-looking people, or people in powerful positions.

The kind of curiosity *we're* suggesting, however, is the curiosity of caring. To notice someone's needs, we have to be interested in that person. That means that our interest doesn't stop when we find out fascinating facts. Interest goes deeper: trying to find out the most precious desires in a person's heart; discovering the most secret and lovely thoughts that a person has been ashamed to tell because he was afraid of ridicule; and finding those holes in a person's life, not to exploit his needs, but rather to fulfil them.

Without that kind of caring, most opportunities to give love and service where they are really needed will pass us by unnoticed.

And it's so easy not to notice even obvious things! For instance, quickly count the number of *f*'s in the next sentence (read it only once): Finished files are the result of years of scientific study combined with the experience of years.

How many *f*'s did you count?

Seventy percent of those who read that sentence see three *f*'s. Actually, however, there are six.

Didn't you get six? Go back and count again. Most people who missed several *f*'s missed them in the simple word *of*, a word so unimportant that our eye just skips right over it. It's a common word: too common for us to make it important without making a special effort.

Far too often we have programmed our brain to overlook certain things, particularly with people we know very well. We simply don't notice some very important things about them, because we think we already know them. And we don't notice many things about strangers because we have programmed our brains to overlook them entirely!

When we spend our lives being inward-directed, or being caught up with only our own pleasures and selfish desires, we leave little time to develop a curiosity toward other people and their lives. We program our brains to shut them out. We do not see their needs, their wants, their feelings. This is perceived as "nonessential" data. Unimportant. Trivia. Our mental computer has no room for data like that.

While we know precisely how much the cost of milk has gone up over the last six months, we don't notice that our child has been coming home from school earlier and staying shut up in his room for a few minutes. It might mean he's lost friends at school and is lonely—but it's "trivial," just a little detail that's easy to miss.

While we know exactly how much the government is withholding from our paycheck, we didn't realize that our spouse is desperately in need of some new clothes—and she's too worried about finances to mention it. The fraying of her collars and the fading of the fabric on her dresses happened too gradually: it's "trivial," and we just don't see it.

We walk along our own Jericho Roads like the priest and the Levite in the parable of the Good Samaritan, closing our eyes to anything we don't really want to see.

And then we look at those select few of our friends and neighbors who always seem to find time to do good things for other people.

"Mrs. Johnson took care of the Kerby kids while their parents went to Houston for Sister Kerby's operation."

"Oh, really? I didn't know she was sick. How does Mrs. Johnson always find out these things?"

Good question. The answer? She cares enough to find out— and then cares enough to *do* something about it.

"But no one ever tells me anything!"

Do you ever stop long enough to notice whether they are trying?

Those who make it their task to find out who is in need of something they can provide, and lovingly give as much as they can—these are outward-directed Christians. And we can't help but feel that people who have learned to become wholly giving are regarded highly by our Heavenly Father—after all, they are the ones who are sharing in his work of bringing as much happiness to his children as they are willing to accept.

President David O. McKay said that serving our fellowman is the highest ideal of religion ever given to man. And King Benjamin affirmed, "Behold, I tell you these things that ye may learn wisdom; that ye may learn that when ye are in the service of your fellow beings ye are only in the service of your God." (Mos. 2:17.)

May we suggest to you a formula for caring—an equation someone has developed that helps us to better understand the results when you care and when you don't:

$$A^1 + A^2 = D$$
$$D \div PC = S \text{ and } H$$

A^1 is *apathy*—lack of caring.

A^2 is *adversity*—which can range from a serious problem to anything even a little out of the ordinary.

Add those together, and you get D: Disaster!

But now divide *disaster* by PC—*people who care*, and the results will be S and H, *success and happiness*.

And the most exciting thing about this formula is that success and happiness aren't just for the person helped, but also for the person helping—and for a lot of other people, too.

If you want that success and happiness, not only for yourself but also for everyone you love, then start now. By caring.

"But I can't make much difference in the amount of happiness in the world," many people say.

You'd be surprised at how much difference one person who cares can make. And to help you understand, in this book we've compiled some stories of acts of caring. We invite you to journey with us into the lives and experiences of other people who found people they could love as they, like the Good Samaritan, passed along the road to Jericho.

Some of the stories are fiction; most are true—like those shown within large quotation marks. All of them, however, are true in the sense that kindness is within your reach. And if you are moved by even one story to care a bit more about someone you might otherwise not have noticed, then the good these people did will live on in *your* good acts, even as your kindness will live on in other people's lives.

For your kindness is a flow of living water: As others' kindnesses fill *you*, your kindness also flows out to fill others, too. And the more you give, the more room you have in your heart to receive.

2

DOGFOOD AND OTHER GIFTS

Gifts. Whenever one person comes in contact with another, however briefly, they each give the other a gift. It may be large or small,
intentional or otherwise, but the gift is still there. You receive
many of them daily, you give away many yourself at the same time.
Have you considered what kinds of gifts you are in the habit of
giving?

❝ "In a testimony meeting I attended not long ago, at the
very end of the service, a girl arose and made her way to the front of
the room where she stood for long moments in silence, her lips
trembling and her eyes overflowing. At last, when she had her
emotions under control, she related to the congregation the following experience:

"Some three years previously, while her father was stationed
with the military in Germany, he had made a thorough study of the
principles of the gospel and at length had joined the Church.
Within a year he was transferred back to the States, and his family
settled in Maryland, where they immediately affiliated with one of
the local wards.

"This young woman, in her teens, found that there were four
other girls in the ward her age, and with great expectations she
looked forward to a close association with them as they all grew in
the knowledge of her so-recently reemphasized gospel.

"Yet she was to discover, quickly and painfully, that the girls
in her new ward had a totally different idea about things. They were
a close group, their families were long-time residents, their fathers
held important ward and stake positions, and they could see no
need to disrupt their unity and established pattern of living by
becoming friends with an 'army brat,' as they called her.

"At first the girls were subtle in their persecutions, snickering when she was brave enough to make a comment in class, ignoring her when she spoke to them, and turning as a group and walking away laughing whenever she approached.

"For a time she tried to ignore their rudeness, assuming that it was because she was new in the ward. She felt that with a little time they would all become good friends. It seemed, though, that she was wrong. Time seemed merely to aggravate and intensify the problems.

"A strong girl, she was initially able to handle the situation emotionally, but after a period of weeks and months she began to wonder what was wrong with her and even to feel that she was the one who was at fault.

"To eliminate the snickering and giggling when she participated in class, she stopped taking part. To keep the girls from pointedly ignoring her when she spoke to them, she quit speaking, at first to them and then almost altogether.

"At school it became the practice of the four girls to call out and jeer in derision whenever she appeared, and it wasn't long before she was slumping down and hiding her face simply so the girls wouldn't notice her. At home her mother worried about her poor posture, but the pattern was established and was not easily changed.

"For a year this ridicule and persecution continued, and it was so intense and so constant that it had a severe impact on her image of herself. If they thought of her as nothing, how could she be anything else?

"Her parents, of course, did all in their power to correct the situation. They went to the parents of each of the girls and talked it over with them, and those parents agreed to help. Yet when they confronted their daughters the girls denied their guilt. And the situation remained unchanged.

"At length, realizing that their daughter was being destroyed emotionally, the girl's parents decided that they would send her west to live with her grandmother. She agreed, and soon the word was around that she was leaving.

"On her last Sunday in the ward, following another rough experience in Sunday School, she went to sacrament meeting as usual. During the meeting she noticed that a counselor in the Relief Society presidency was having trouble with her baby, so she took the child and tended it out in the foyer, thus freeing the woman to listen to the service.

"As the meeting ended and people began filling up the foyer the four girls ran breathlessly up to her. They were all smiles and cheer and bubbly enthusiasm, and as she searched their radiant faces and listened to their expressions of sorrow that she was leaving she found it difficult to contain her emotions.

"Was it possible? Could it be that after a whole year they were finally changing? She held the fussing baby and wondered aloud that they were suddenly interested in her.

"The girls giggled and assured her that of course they were concerned. They felt badly about Sunday School and had all gone in together to purchase her a going-away present. That, if anything ever could, would prove their concern for her, and tell her how they really felt about her.

"She was so astounded that she stood mute while they handed her a gift, beautifully wrapped, and then scurried away. She was still standing silently, gazing in awe at the present, when the counselor came after her baby.

"She too noticed the brightly wrapped gift and so stood excitedly near as the girl carefully untied the bows and unwrapped the paper. And as she unwrapped it she was struggling with her tears. It was incredibly wonderful that the girls had finally changed. She had waited so long and had tried so hard and had been rebuffed so many times—but it had finally worked out.

"At last she had the paper open, and as she gazed down into the box she could hold her tears back no longer, and they fell freely as she stood quietly and sobbed out her feelings.

"The Relief Society counselor, silently wondering at the girl's burst of emotion, leaned over so that she might also observe, and there she saw, carefully placed in that beautifully wrapped package, the girl's gift from her friends, from her Latter-day Saint friends.

"And she too felt the tears start in her own eyes, for inside the box the girl was holding was a can of dogfood." **"**

Now, quickly, lest we think the above is an isolated example, consider the following true experience:

" "I went to school in a small town here in Utah, and it was really hard because the girls were, well, mean. Now I don't really blame them, because that was kind of how they were raised. It is a very small town, and the Church just isn't important to those kids. Their attitude was, Try everything once.

"But I wanted to be different; I just didn't believe like they did.

My dad was my sixth grade teacher, and that made it really hard, both for him and for me, because he could see how they were always trying to make me do things I shouldn't.

"I had one girl friend who was always doing things wrong, and yet somehow I usually got the blame. So I didn't think too much of myself. Even though I was mostly innocent, I felt mostly guilty.

"So in the eighth grade my parents sent me to another town to go to school, and I just loved it there. I lived with my aunt and later my grandparents. And I had a lot of friends, and I guess they helped me get back my self-esteem. But I hated going home. I mean, I loved my own family but no one else accepted me like I wanted to be. You know. I wanted to be part of the Church, I wanted to live the gospel, and they were always putting me down for it.

"Anyway, one of the teachers that year in my home town had all the kids write me letters as a Christmas present, and I guess the teacher didn't read the letters or something, because when I got them I remember how awful they were. I cried a lot, I know that.

"Lots of them blamed my Dad for me being like I was, and they wanted me to deny everything I stood for and then I could come back and they would be my friends again. They told me that the Church wasn't that important, and that if I did anything that turned out to be wrong then, well, I could always repent later.

"By this time most of the kids back home who had written me were smoking and drinking, a lot of the girls and guys had moral problems, and it was pretty bad. But their letters affected me for a long time, and I was nearly out of high school before I could see that they were really just being small people. I could finally see right through everything they tried to do to me, and so could everyone else around us. All but them." **99**

Kindness or dogfood or anti-Christian essays are all good and bad gifts given by Heavenly Father's children to each other. Which kind of gift do *we* give?

Two young men come to mind, two students who sat through different years in the same seminary classroom. The first, as a young boy, had been hit by an automobile. He recovered, but suffered enough brain damage to permanently impair his motor nerves. His thinking was if anything quicker than most others', but his speech was slurred and his bodily actions jerky.

One day in class, after his attempt to participate was met with a great deal of snickering and mockery, the instructor sent the young man out on an errand and then in a very literal way told the class what he thought of the way they had acted.

12

Yet little changed, and eventually the young man graduated from school and was called on a mission. Nearly a year later a letter arrived at the seminary, addressed to his teacher. He opened it and read the briefest of notes:

"Dear Brother—:

"I'm so busy that I don't have time to write, but I did want to thank you for helping me to learn about our glorious gospel. Being a missionary is the greatest thing I have ever done. I love the Lord with all my heart.

"Love,

"P.S. I don't have time to write another letter, so would you please give this letter to Rocky and Adelle?

"Dear Rocky and Adelle:

"I just wanted to write you and thank you for being the only two friends I ever had in school. Someday I hope you will know how much your friendship has meant to me. May God bless both of you always.

"Love,"

Can you imagine that? Twelve years of school in an LDS community and only two friends? Only two of his peers had not, on a consistent basis, given him cans of dogfood. And it should be added that, according to his mission president, he was the most successful missionary in the mission.

Now to the other young man, a slightly built fellow who said little and was not—well, socially adept. In fact, he had one or two habits that were most assuredly anti-social, or at least seemed calculated to drive any well-mannered person away.

Yet in seminary one morning, when this boy was absent, a beautiful girl, one of the sweetest in the class, stood in devotional and challenged the whole class to overlook his offensive habits and go out of their way to treat him as a special person. The class enthusiastically followed her lead and example, and the balance of that year was a very special one for all involved.

Then, on the last day of school, as the students were standing and expressing their feelings, this boy stood up also. For a moment or two he struggled with his emotions, and then quickly he thanked the class for making him feel so good and well-liked during the year. And then, in a quiet voice, he made a statement that no one in that class will ever forget. He said, "In fact, it is because of you kids that I decided last night after my personal prayer that I want to be baptized."

Isn't that interesting? No one in the class, including the seminary teacher, had the foggiest idea that he wasn't a member. But you can bet that there were some thankful sighs that they had influenced him for good rather than otherwise.

Because of the efforts of one girl and a willing class who cared enough to give the gift of friendship, that young man is now almost through with his own mission.

By now you will no doubt have thought of gifts you have given, or perhaps gifts that you can give. Emerson said it well when he said, "Rings and jewels are not gifts, but apologies for gifts. The only true gift is a portion of thyself."

Remember this very morning, when you either smiled or didn't smile at a particular person? Try it now, while you're sitting there. First of all, make the biggest frown you can possibly make, then, switch it over and smile the happiest smile you can spread across your face. Can you imagine the difference in your feelings from the frown to the smile? And if you feel that way, knowing that neither of them is real anyway, then think how someone else, a friend, a family member, or even just a stranger, must feel when they see you either frowning or smiling in earnest.

A friend of ours likes to walk down the street in Salt Lake City smiling for all he is worth. He tells us that his smile takes no longer than a minute to become real simply because of the amusing reactions of others, which go all the way from people turning away to many who smile back to some who even stop to chat, thinking they must know him from somewhere, if they could just remember where.

And what about kind words? Have you thought much about the value of that gift? Here's an experience of Blaine's:

In seminary a few years ago I noticed a student who seemed really down, and this discouragement persisted for several days. Finally, on this particular day, I left the classroom and found another teacher. "Tell me," I said, "something good about so-and-so." That teacher, a wise man, quickly understood and told me three or four very praiseworthy things about my student. I then walked back into class, waited a few moments, and suddenly noticed the student.

"Hey, do you know that I heard some of the neatest things about you today."

"Huh?"

Repeat.

"Are you talking to me?"

14

"Sure I am. Isn't your name so-and-so?"

"Yeah."

"Then I'm talking to you."

"What'd ya hear?"

"Oh, I can't say, but it was all good. Very good, in fact."

"Who said it then?"

"I can't tell you, but I can tell you that it was an adult, and I can tell you, too, that he surely has a high opinion of you."

"Come on, Brother Yorgason, tell me!"

"Oh, no, but be proud, because I sure would be if someone said that about me."

Well, you can imagine the effect that conversation had on that kid that day. He left the room floating on a cloud, and since he didn't know who said what, he was nice to everyone for hours.

In the years since then I have done that many times to adults as well as kids, and the effects have always been very remarkable.

Another great gift is the gift of time, and for many it is the most difficult of all gifts to give. Have you time for your parents? Have you time for your children? Have you time to do your home teaching or visiting teaching? Do you take time to care for the lonely and helpless? The apostle James (James 1:27) tells us that this gift of time is pure and undefiled religion before God.

There are gifts of the heart, such as kindness, joy, understanding, sympathy, tolerance, forgiveness. . . .

Gifts of the spirit, which would include prayer, vision, beauty, aspiration, peace of heart, faith. . . .

Gifts of the mind, such as ideas, dreams, purposes, ideals, plans, inventions, projects, music, prose and poetry. . . .

All such gifts ease the heart of the recipient and lighten the burden he has been called to bear. And they also gladden the giver, giving him, for just a moment at least, a glimpse into the heart of our Father in heaven, who "so loved the world, that he gave his only begotten Son, that whosoever believeth in him should not perish, but have everlasting life." (John 3:16.)

In the Yorgason family folklore there is an interesting story about our great-grandfather, who had eight wives. It is said that about two days before he was to visit with one of his wives she would make a big pot of stew. Then for two days straight she would boil it down so that by the time he arrived everything in the pot would have "boiled down to pure nourishment." She seemed to feel that he needed all the strength he could get.

Let us liken this little tale to all the possible good gifts that we may give others. If we could put them all in a pot and boil them down, when we finished we would find nothing in the bottom of the pot but love. Love is what all other good gifts finally come to.

The apostle Paul gave a great discourse on the subject of pure love, or charity, in which he said:

Charity suffereth long, and is kind; charity envieth not; charity vaunteth not itself, is not puffed up,

Doth not behave itself unseemly, seeketh not her own, is not easily provoked, thinketh no evil;

Rejoiceth not in iniquity, but rejoiceth in the truth;

Beareth all things, believeth all things, hopeth all things, endureth all things.

And now abideth faith, hope, charity, these three; but the greatest of these is charity. (1 Cor. 13:4-7, 13.)

Can you tell what Paul has done here? In effect, he has analyzed love. He has broken it down into its basic components so that we might recognize more fully which qualities we need in our lives:

1. Patience: "Charity suffereth long."
2. Kindness: "And is kind."
3. Trust: "Love envieth not."
4. Humility: "Love vaunteth not itself, is not puffed up."
5. Courtesy: "Doth not behave itself unseemly."
6. Unselfishness: "Seeketh not her own."
7. Good Temper: "Is not easily provoked."
8. Guilelessness: "Thinketh no evil."
9. Sincerity: "Rejoiceth not in iniquity, but rejoiceth in the truth."

Go through these nine qualities in your mind. Aren't you impressed with how your life might change if you were to adopt each of them? For instance, if you had the quality of patience, can you imagine how relationships would improve just in your family? And how about the quality of courtesy? If we all showed perfect courtesy toward other people there would be no crime, there would be no immorality, there would be no hurt feelings.

Wouldn't our world be fantastic if we just had these *two* qualities, let alone all nine of them, to give to others?

In Matthew 25, Jesus depicts our final judgment with the image of a ruler sitting upon a throne dividing the sheep from the goats, placing the sheep on his right hand and the goats on his left. He tells those on his right hand to come with him to the kingdom prepared for them from before the foundation of the world, and beginning in verse 35 he explains the criteria by which they were chosen.

Boiled down to its final ingredients, the test is not "How have I believed?" but rather "How have I loved? How have I cared? What gifts have I given?"

The final test of our religion, then, is not religiousness, but love. It is the giving of ourselves to others.

What gifts will you give tomorrow?

3

LEARNING TO LOVE OURSELVES

The sun was sloping down the western sky when the old buzzard, in its endless circling, first saw movement. Dropping lower and extending its primaries to slow its speed the buzzard was quickly able to determine that the movement it had seen was the hand of a man, barely visible beyond the brush that hid the rest of his body from sight.

The old buzzard, the undertaker of the desert, knew that movement meant life, and that in turn meant that the man under the bush was not yet his business. Tomorrow maybe, but not now. For now, he could wait. There were other meals less risky, and the old buzzard never took risks. That was why he was an old buzzard, old and healthy. So on he drifted, silent as death, and the man on the ground had no knowledge even of his passing.

Again the man moved, straining his eyes, lifting his head with a monumental effort to determine which direction offered him the most hope. But in all directions the land stretched the same, barren and blistered and hopelessly dry. Heat waves shimmered their veil across the distance. A few cottony puffballs of cloud hung against the brassy afternoon sky, and perspiration trickled down his body. Before him strange dust-devils played across the face of the land, and above the mirage of a distant blue lake the heads of the cedars peered like strange beings from some alien world.

The man, his eyes red-rimmed from sun-glare, his face whitened by alkali and his muscles heavy with weariness, rose awkwardly to his feet. He swayed then, trying to focus his eyes, gathering his failing strength that he might continue his endless and seemingly hopeless march. His body smelled of stale sweat, his clothing was stiff with sweat and dust, and he tried to focus his mind, to remember whether it had been two days or three since his plane had crashed.

Pain gnawed at his side like a hungry animal . . . such a little wound, but it needed care, it needed cleansing. Only there was no water to cleanse it with, no water to sooth his parched lips and throat, no water anywhere to do anything with. . . .

In his mouth he carried a pebble. He had heard that it helped relieve thirst, and he hoped that it would, but so far he couldn't tell that it had helped very much.

He worked his jaws. His brain throbbed heavily and when he shifted his gaze his eyeballs grated dryly in their sockets, moving with painful slowness. Just like all the rest of his body. Slow, painfully slow.

For an hour he moved forward into the afternoon, inching his way across the broken land, picking his path carefully around giant clinkers of lava left by ancient volcanic upheavals. He crawled occasionally, stumbled along upright when he could, and yet always he moved northwesterly, his goal a faint blue against the sky, a range of mountains that looked cool, so invitingly cool, and yet so everlastingly far away.

His mind worked now with startling clarity, yet he distrusted it, knowing this clarity was the beginning of delirium. He felt his weakness, knowing he needed rest, water, and time to clean his wound.

In him was no self-pity, no self-condemnation for being there. He had done what had to be done, had done his best to complete his mission, and when the plane engine had died he had brought it down as best he was able. That he was alive attested to the fact that his crash-landing had been a good one. Yet there had been no emergency rations in the plane, and no water. That was his fault. He should have checked that before he left. But he hadn't, and he must think now of tomorrow, not of yesterday.

The red ball of the sun slid behind the horizon, and almost instantly, it seemed to the man, the desert was dark. Dark and cold. He now experienced the contradiction of the desert, and as he chilled he wondered that it could get so cold so fast. His head throbbed heavily. His mouth was dry, his lips parched and broken. He had a fever . . . he could feel it, and he was shaking uncontrollably in the cold. His wound was dirty and he could feel the gnawing agony of it constantly. His hands felt unnaturally large and his head was heavy and awkward.

Yet through the night he moved forward, slowly slowly forward. There were passages of delirium then, passages through which were woven thin threads of sanity. Thus in the light of morning, when he saw the footprints in the bed of the desert wash along which he was crawling, he was able to recognize them for what they were. For an hour he followed them, stumbling and crawling forward as rapidly as he could, hoping almost without hope that he could catch the man, that he. . . .

The first thing he saw were the boots, standing together on the floor of the wash. With an effort he lifted his eyes, following up the man's legs, up. . . .

"Hey," said a voice. "Hey! Do you need a drink? You look terrible. You look like . . . "

"Water . . ." the man managed to croak.

"Sure, sure, got my canteen right here. Yes, I never go into the desert without my canteen. Here it is."

And the dying man struggled with the cap, forced it open at last with his feeble fingers, and put the mouth of the canteen to his parched lips and drank.

No, *tried* to drink. But there was nothing in the canteen, nothing but air.

"Doggone," said the man who would help. "Guess I forgot to fill it before I left home."

You can't give someone a drink unless you have some water yourself!

We (the authors) know a woman who, all her life, has had a tremendous sense of empathy and sympathy for the downtrodden, the unfortunate souls of this world. When she sees an individual in distress or in agony of body or spirit, it is in her nature to feel that agony with them and to desire to help them out of it. Yet, most unfortunately, she has never prepared herself to help others in any way but superficially. Thus when she goes to the aid of someone whose soul is in torment, instead of quenching their thirst and lifting them up, in a very short time this woman finds herself crawling along in the dust of dismay right alongside the one she so desired to help.

We are told to love God first and foremost, and then to love our neighbors as unstintingly as we love ourselves. Now that sounds easy enough, until we realize just how many people there are who simply do not like themselves at all. How can these people, who care nothing for themselves, ever fulfill the commandment to love their neighbor?

This lack of love for self is called by many names: low self-esteem, low self-confidence, lack of self-assurance and self-reliance, insecurity. Whatever the title we give it, the problem seems most always to develop or at least begin in childhood:

> The fundamental skill required of anyone who handles children, is learning to get behind the eyes of a child—to feel what he feels and know what he is experiencing. In general, children are particularly sensitive about their physical attractiveness and their basic ability or intelligence. Anything which makes them feel ugly or dumb, or embarrasses them in front of others, tends to weaken self-esteem.
>
> When important adults in a child's life are disappointed in him, a child soon knows. If adults learn to recognize their own attitudes, this, in itself, is a big step in dealing with them.
>
> Children need to feel both loved and respected. You can love them enough to die for them and yet not view them with respect.
>
> When your child speaks out in front of company, do you tend to jump in and try to explain what he's trying to say? Or laugh nervously? Or send him away? Does your youngster get the impression you find it a difficult task to make him look attractive? Children are amazingly perceptive at reading the emotional messages behind our words and actions. (James Dobson, Ph.D., associate clinical professor of pediatrics at University of Southern California School of Medicine, as quoted in Provo *Daily Herald*, November 24, 1977.)

One situation that seems to contribute very heavily to feelings of inadequacy in children is the broken home. In 1977 the Utah State Division of Alcoholism and Drugs conducted a survey among three thousand high school students throughout the state, and they found, among other things, a significant correlation between low self-esteem and drug and alcohol abuse. Interestingly, they found, too, that a high percentage of kids who used drugs and alcohol came from single-parent homes. Troubled homes may well be a primary cause of children's self-doubt.

Consider one young person's experience:

" "When my mother was a small child her parents decided that they could never be happy with each other, and so they divorced. My mother stayed with her mother, but there wasn't enough money and so my mother was placed in a school that took care of children without parents. She grew up feeling that no one cared about her or liked her, and it wasn't too hard for her to convince herself that she really wasn't worth liking.

22

"Well, then she met my Father and was married, and no matter how many times he told her that he loved her, or how many ways he showed her that he did, she would not believe him. How could he really love a person like she was, she asked herself? Nobody could really love her. So she was a very lonely and unhappy woman surrounded by a family who really did love her. At some point she started drinking, and as she found escape in alcohol she depended more on it until she became an alcoholic.

"Shortly after I left home to get married she asked my father for a divorce. He came to me about the divorce, grief-stricken because he could not convince his wife, my mother, of his and our love for her. They did get the divorce, and now when we see my mother, who is still an alcoholic, she tells us that she doesn't blame us for not loving her. And she says that even when we tell her that we really do. Because she doesn't love herself, she can't understand it when somebody else tries.

"I was lucky that I was older when they separated, but my younger brother wasn't so fortunate. He too felt the same kinds of feelings of insecurity that my mother had felt when she was younger, and so he went the whole bad scene, drugs and everything, trying to find—oh, I don't know what he was trying to find. Happiness, I guess. Just someone who could really love him. He's doing much better now. He still isn't active in the Church, but he is such a fine man, and we love him very much." **"**

Carrying this theme a bit further, consider for a moment the following account, beautifully written, delightfully humorous, and yet pathetic, nevertheless, because of the insight it provides:

" " 'Step up on the scales, please.'
" 'I beg your pardon?'
" 'The scales. We've got to get your weight; it's part of the physical.'
" 'Oh, uh—I can't.'
" 'Why not?'
" 'Uh, I'm afraid of heights?'
" 'Miss Miller, please!'
"Suddenly all the candy, cookies, doughnuts, and double chili-cheeseburgers I had ever eaten were piled in one oppressive heap at the bottom of my stomach. I turned my head casually to see if my high-school friends were watching. They were.
" 'Part of the physical my puffy eye,' I thought. 'This is just the way the cheerleading supervisors get their kicks.'

"I stepped on the scale. I knew then how Marie Antoinette had felt when they placed her head in the guillotine. I wished my head had been cut off. It would have lightened my weight considerably.

"The nurse's small hands fidgeted endlessly with the weights. Such torment! I felt like a prize pig on its way to the fair.

" 'One hundred sixty-two pounds!'

"How such a loud booming voice could issue from such a frail frame I'll never know, but the nurse's words echoed explosively through the small drab office.

"Why don't you just use a P.A. system, I thought bitterly, at the same time wishing that she'd contract a severe case of laryngitis. The recorder seemed to smirk repulsively as she jotted down my statistics in the book, and then I was excused, leaving my friends alone to giggle.

"So started the week's competition for cheerleading tryouts. My routine was solid, full of gymnastics, kicks, all the winning elements, I thought. But what little confidence I had managed to build up had been shattered somewhere in the nurse's office. Possibly a six-day fast? Or maybe an East Indian body transplant? No, I knew the only answer was to rely on my talent and my friendliness. Perhaps everyone would overlook my dimpled thighs and pudgy cheeks, and by chance the 'Rubens look' might be in by the end of the week.

"Friday came quickly, bringing a chill in the air that even an oversized coat couldn't appease. I walked down the corridor and nervously studied the faces of my classmates. There were Sheila and Margy and Fran—I had always been nice to them. And there was Tom Simpson, the junior class president. How I had delighted in helping him with his campaign the year before, just to be close to him. I recalled how the scent of his aftershave mingled with that of the magic marker as we compiled a myriad number of posters expounding his many qualifications. Surely he'd vote for me.

"The day passed slowly but I knew that I had performed well that afternoon in front of the studentbody. All stunts were executed flawlessly, and as I had concluded my routine with a spectacular split I heard hoards of applause that seemed to soothe the throbbing pain in my tired body. I had even begun to ponder what name I would choose to embroider on my cheerleading sweater, Susan, Suzie, Sue. . . .

"I ran into Tom Simpson near the voting booth at the end of the day.

24

" 'Hi handsome.'

" 'Hiya Suz, did a real good job today.'

" 'Thanks. Hey, Tom, I know this isn't much of my business, but can I ask you who you voted for?'

" 'Sure. Vicki.'

" 'Vicki!' My heart was in my throat. Somehow it had found its way there through all of the cholesterol.

" 'Yeah, have you *looked* at her? Wow."

"I feigned a good-bye smile. I felt sick about the results of the contest even before they were announced that afternoon. I had missed getting on the squad by ten votes. Maybe if I had been just ten pounds lighter—

"Oh well, somehow it didn't matter. I knew I would never amount to much—except on a scale, of course. What's on the inside doesn't really count at all. These terrible thoughts stayed with me for years. I grew bitter and sarcastic and had such a low opinion of myself that it ate at me nonstop, day and night, all the time." **"**

We will finish Susie's story a little later. For now, though, let us point out that while she is able to look back with humor at this and other incidents in her life, at the time they were not only real, but terrifyingly so. Interestingly, she too came from a broken home.

There are, of course, people who struggle with low self-esteem who come from wonderful homes, and from homes which range all the way from wonderful to miserable and yet are not broken. So obviously that is not the only answer. Nor is it only children who struggle with a low self-concept. Men and women of all ages and backgrounds seem to suffer from this destructive malady.

A man with little formal education may feel inferior to those around him who have achieved mightily in the area of education, even though he is a skilled craftsman whose work is every whit as important in day-to-day living as theirs, and perhaps more so under some circumstances.

Consider the multitudes of men and women who in their entire lives are never called to fill a publicly viewable Church position, such as bishop or elders quorum president or Relief Society president. They spend their whole lives teaching in an auxiliary organization, considering themselves lost in some obscure classroom and feeling inferior to those who are called to positions more prominent. And this even when we read in Mark 1:38 that Christ himself, the greatest of all, was sent forth from the Father to be a teacher. Please consider the following true account:

66 . "I was teaching a class of Sunbeams (three years old) and loved every minute of it. They were so sweet and innocent, and loved any little thing you'd do for them. One day after Primary, a mother of a shy boy in my class came in as I was erasing the chalkboard. We talked a few minutes and then she said that last week after Primary her little boy was telling her what he had learned in Primary and he said, 'Mom, do you know what? My teacher looks just like an angel.'

"From that moment on, I decided in my heart that I would truly teach my class as an angel of God. At times with this class, I had felt that it wasn't important to prepare because the kids were too young to remember anyway, but from this experience I learned the importance of maybe touching the lives of these kids, if only in a small way as with this young boy." **99**

It has been said that in the final judgment Heavenly Father won't ask us which positions we held—but will ask how we fulfilled the positions we have held.

Think for a moment how many feel useless, worn out, in the way, or no good anymore. This problem is especially acute among the elderly, and is beautifully illustrated in this prayer, written by Elise Maclay.

> I feel I'm in the way.
> Nonsense, I am in the way,
> Though the family tells me I'm not.
> No sense priding myself in not making demands.
> They have to help me dress, bathe, follow the conversation.
> They have to take me to the doctor.
> They can't leave me alone without worrying.
> And they have to look at me and see, beyond the ugliness of
>   my wrinkled face and wavering hands, the specter of their
>   own deterioration.
> The young people, of course, don't believe they will ever be
>   old.
> But I am often an embarrassment to them.
> They try to remember the way I used to be and pay homage to
>   that.
> They don't know that I am here, imprisoned in old age, trying
>   to make contact with the world.
> What can I do, Lord? What should I do?
> I love them and long to communicate with them and cannot
>   bear to be in the way.
> Is there something You can teach them through me?

Is there something You want me to learn?
Help me, Lord, to understand why I am still here.
(Elise Maclay, *Green Winter*, New York: Reader's Digest Press, 1977. Used with permission.)

Many of us experience feelings of inadequacy when we observe any form of greatness in another. When we see a beautiful painting we say something like, "Golly, I wish I could paint like that. Why, I can't even draw a straight line." When we observe someone who has developed his talents with music doing a commendable job we wistfully say, "Yeah, and I don't even play the radio well."

Isn't it interesting how we nearly always relate the accomplishments of other people to ourselves? And judge ourselves according to their achievements? And so feel inferior because we do not do as well in that field as they?

Nowhere in the scriptures does it say that we all must become great orators because Joseph Smith was one, or great organizers because Brigham Young had that ability. We can't all paint like Arnold Friberg or play the organ like Alexander Schreiner, and it is wrong to allow ourselves to feel inferior when we can't. The scriptures say there is only one man that we should emulate, and that is Jesus Christ himself. We may use the accomplishments of others as goals in our own lives if we wish, and strive to achieve as they have, but it is only Christ that we should daily strive to become exactly like.

In the Old Testament we have an excellent illustration of this concept. Young David had gone to King Saul with his offer to fight the giant Goliath. Saul, in desperation, had agreed, and in an effort to help had offered David the use of his own personal armor. David obediently put the armor on, only to find that it was so heavy and cumbersome that he was almost unable to move, let alone fight. Removing it, and going to battle armed only with his slingshot and his faith, David slew Goliath and left us with a powerful lesson: It is never wise to engage in the battle of life wearing someone else's armor, trying to be like someone else.

As young boys both of us (the authors) struggled a great deal with feelings of inferiority and inability. Our mother spent endless hours working with us, helping us to develop what she chose to call an inner citadel, a place of refuge within each of us that would always be there, always secure against the storms of life.

Growing up near the ocean in British Columbia, Canada, Mother learned a great deal about the sea. She has told us many times that the fury of storm and wind agitates only the surface of the

27

sea, and never penetrates deeper than two or three hundred feet. Below that is the calm unruffled citadel of the sea, always serene despite the storms raging on the surface. That, she would tell us again and again, was what we needed to develop.

Both Dad and Mother taught all of us self-confidence by giving us plenty to do that they knew we *could*, with effort, do. And then, realizing that self-confidence without self-reliance is as useless as a recipe without the ingredients, they gave us a great deal of freedom to make mistakes and so learn how to accomplish our assigned tasks. In that way we learned to rely upon ourselves.

For instance, we recall many cold mornings when one of us would be carrying the pail of milk the two miles from our corral to our home when the bucket would simply become too heavy. Now, there were probably many ways of solving that problem, but we often chose the easiest and "lost" some of the milk on the way.

Little was ever said, but the next time we were thirsty we had water, and the next time we had hot cereal for breakfast we ate it without milk. Mom and Dad used to call it learning self-reliance the hard way.

Self-reliance, they would tell us, is essential. Self-confidence sees the possibilities; self-reliance molds them into realities. In other words, we are here to work out our own salvation. The individual who is not self-reliant, no matter how astute and intelligent he is, remains weak, hesitating, and doubting of his own abilities in all he does.

Now, self-reliance is not conceit. It is simply daring to stand alone, being an oak, not a vine, being ourselves, not someone else. If people have certain qualities you like, then emulate those qualities, don't try to make yourself over in that person's image. If you would learn to converse well, put yourself in positions where you must speak. If you would conquer depression, mingle with the bright and happy people around you, no matter how difficult it may be. If you desire an ability that someone else possesses, do not envy it and dissipate your strength by weakly wishing his ability were yours. Emulate the process by which it became his. Be self-reliant. Pay the price he paid and that ability will be yours also.

Blaine has a good friend in Rexburg, Idaho, Don Ricks, who is an outstanding artist. Occasionally Blaine has heard people say to him, "You know, I'd give my right arm to paint like you do." His comment has always been that a right arm isn't necessary. Thirty years or so would do just fine, for that is the price that he has paid.

Self-reliance doesn't mean, of course, that we conceive of

ourselves as being absolutely alone in the world. In fact, we do depend on other people for many things—for love, for affection, for conversation, for learning. It's a foolish person who thinks that he is completely self-made.

But it is just as foolish a person who thinks that he can do nothing to make himself! And that is the key to self-reliance: to do all that we can to make ourselves excellent in every area we care to excel in, and then trust in others to supply the needs we can't supply ourselves.

After all, self-reliance, all alone, doesn't get you very far in the eternal scheme—we must rely on Christ to get us into the celestial kingdom. Yet Christ's sacrifice does us no good unless we rely on ourselves to reach out and accept his gift.

So we have to think and act as if all good things in our future depended on our own actions, and as if all good things in our past were a gift from God. And, of course, we have to believe that we are capable of the achievements we set out for.

Dad used to say all this in just one sentence: "You can't get up a hill by thinking downhill thoughts."

Yet the positive mental attitude is only a start—and not a very profitable one, if we don't know what to do next to "fill up our canteens."

My casual acquaintance on the train that was speeding across that autumn landscape seemed thoughtful, reflective, a little wistful as we talked about the things we saw from the car window. At last we came to a big meadow wherein were grazing half a hundred beef cattle. I said something inane about the prosperity of the country, the glowing future of the livestock industry, and so forth. "Look at those little daisies," he said, pointing to a bright patch of them in a far corner of the meadow. Then he added, "Cattle somehow can't thrill me. There's more hope for humanity in a wild flower than in tons of beef."

Long after he left me, I kept thinking of what he had said, wondering just what he had meant. His idea, of course, is that a wild flower is one of life's extras, one of those things we do not *have* to have but which we enjoy all the more for that very reason.

The more I thought about this, the more it appeared that Creation supplies us with only two kinds of things: necessities and extras. Sunlight, air, water, food, shelter—these are among the bare necessities. With them we can exist. But moonlight and starlight are distinctly extras; so are music, the perfumes, flowers. The wind is perhaps a necessity; but the song that it croons through the morning pines is a different thing. (Archibald Rutledge, *Life's Extras*, Flemming H. Revell Company, 1961.)

Heavenly Father loves us and cares about us enough to give us all we need. This includes, of course, the gospel of Jesus Christ, the plan he has given us which, if followed, will enable each of us to return to his presence through the sacrifice which his Son made for us.

Of course we have our agency, and if we wish may choose to ignore the importance of the gift which Heavenly Father has given us. However, we are not free of the consequences of disobedience.

We have the freedom to stuff our minds full of whatever kinds of things we choose to stuff them full of, good or bad; but whatever we sow there will eventually have to be harvested. Our friend Max Walters has written: "One cannot watch the arc of a welder with the naked eye without severe pain, probably some damage and possibly after enough time, blindness. The same results occur when staring directly into the sun. The pain these examples cause, however, is almost always delayed—hours, days, weeks, and maybe months and years.

"Only a man void of the Spirit and ignorant as pertaining to the laws of God will not recognize that the same kind of damage occurs when he views or hears pornography, in any of its forms. The pain from such exposure is usually not felt immediately, nor is it immediately apparent that his spiritual vision has been impaired. Yet it has, and that pain will be felt and the damage noticed either at some point where repentance occurs or else at the Bar of God when the time to repent has passed and he is found guilty in his sins."

We can go through each of the other commandments, but the results will be the same. When we break one of them, in one way or another we lose a little freedom.

The deepest self-love, the most profound self-respect, the greatest amount of self-reliance, will come only to those who understand the gospel of Jesus Christ and whose lives are in harmony with his teachings. In this way only will your own canteen of water be full enough that you may give to others to drink.

Remember back now to the story about Susie, who tried out for the cheerleading team and didn't make it? Let's now read the rest of her account, remembering as we do that she was struggling desperately to like herself—even a little bit.

" "The low opinion I had of myself continued nonstop until one day I heard a prophet of the Lord speak to a group of college students. He spoke of the divine worth of every living soul, and of how all of us are children of Heavenly Parents. He told of the love Heavenly Father feels for us individually, and that we are all precious in his sight. He also said we could live with him again if we were willing to live righteously.

"Suddenly my pounds of depression and self-pity seemed a lighter load. I became a member of The Church of Jesus Christ of Latter-day Saints, and my confidence grew along with my self-control. My happiness and inner peace became strengthened. In fact, everything about me grew but my waistline, which along with my soul became a figure of delight. I will never attain a position on the cheerleading squad. But the sweetness of knowing that I am valuable, that I am loved, far surpasses even the richest culinary delights."

Isn't it interesting how the gospel affects the lives of the people who become involved with it? Once an individual begins to understand who he or she really is, that they are truly offspring of God with at least a spark of divinity in each of them, how can they help but grow in self-esteem, self-confidence, and self-reliance?

"For me, learning to love myself began at the waters of baptism. I was eighteen when I received a testimony of the validity of the LDS faith, after having spent a year of spiritual struggle and turmoil as a Catholic at BYU.

"Receiving a testimony of the truthfulness of the restoration, realizing that I am a daughter of the Almighty God, and pondering that 'as man is, God once was, and as God is, man may become' has enabled me to learn to love and to look at myself in a very different light.

"Full of inferiority complexes and tendencies toward serious depressive states and so on when I came to BYU, I found there that humility is not self-destruction. I forced myself as I recognized this to take speech and drama classes to help me overcome my great fear of public speaking, relying on the Lord for the strength I needed to meet each personal challenge geared toward improvement of myself.

"I found this quote and carried it with me: 'I can do all things through Christ, which strengtheneth me.' And now as a wife and a mother I find more than ever that I must lean heavily on the Spirit of Christ to enable me to perform and to love my family and myself as he loves me."

31

So we come back down to the admonition of Christ, to love our neighbors *as much as we love ourselves.* This two-part commandment cannot be divided in order to be observed. For us to thoroughly love others, to care for them and their needs, we must first be satisfied with our own lives. We must be comfortable with ourselves physically, mentally, emotionally and, especially, spiritually. Only then, when all these things are taken care of, will we have our canteens full enough to maximize our ability to share with others. Christlike caring can be done in no other way:

> But whosoever drinketh of the water that I shall give him shall never thirst; but the water that I shall give him shall be in him a well of water springing up into everlasting life. (John 4:14).

4

CHOCOLATE MILK AND DONUTS

❝ "During elementary school and high school, I was very shy—almost reclusive. It was not until my first year of college that I began to gain confidence and begin the long trek out of my social shell.

"It was upon my return to Rexburg for my sophomore year that I moved in with a new group of girls. We immediately felt a closeness as we set up housekeeping and prepared for a new school year together. It is difficult to express my anxieties of acceptance as I fought the feelings of inferiority which for so many years had plagued me.

"It was not until my roommates began to center their conversations around boys and dating that I began to climb back into my shell. Up to that point in my life I had never been on a date. I had no idea what it was like to have a boyfriend, go to a formal dance, write to a missionary, or have any of the experiences so vital to a young girl in college. I began to feel left out of their conversations, and thus became very distant from them, and very lonely.

"It was a bright and cheerful Saturday morning that I decided I had to get out of the apartment, as I was anything but bright and cheerful. And so I began my journey across town to the hospital where my sister was working. When I arrived I felt embarrassed with my red eyes, runny nose, and tears streaming down my face, and so I simply sat in her car and cried even more.

"When she finished her shift she was quite surprised to find me sitting in her car crying. I'll never forget the way she climbed in, slid across the seat, and took me in her arms. After comforting me for what seemed like an eternity, she asked, 'What's the matter, Sis?' I was crying so much I could hardly talk, but she listened intently for over an hour as I poured out the anxieties and feelings of my heart.

"And then, instead of telling me what I should do or how to rid myself of the feelings I had, my dear sister simply said, 'I think we need to go for a ride.'

"With that, she started the car, backed out of the parking lot, and we were off to Idaho Falls. As we drove into town, we spotted a little country store, and so we stopped and in she went. When she came out moments later, she was carrying some donuts and chocolate milk. Without saying a word, we wound our way through the city until we came to a park overlooking the Idaho Falls Temple.

"As we stretched out on the grass and began to eat our chocolate milk and donuts, Sis expressed her love for me, and told me how special she thought I was. It was just what the doctor ordered as we talked about many of our early childhood experiences, and before long we were both laughing and goofing around.

"This was a very special experience for me, as I knew that Sis really cared about me and loved me for what I am. She helped me change my attitude and start out my best year of college right—a year which would hold all those experiences I so desperately wanted and could later share with my roommates.

"This was only the first of what we have come to cherish as many 'chocolate milk and donut' moments . . . moments when caring and lifting are all that seem to matter."   **"**

The world around us gets the tail wagging the dog where love is concerned. It is fashionable to think of love and loving as does Winch, who states, "We love those who satisfy our needs."

We prefer to turn that around: "We satisfy the needs of those we love."

Do you see the difference? One definition of love does not involve itself with caring and giving, but rather centers around selfish fulfillment and personal gratification.

Look at yourself. Perhaps you have, to some degree, adopted the world's selfish definition of love. Such people and families are pretty easy to identify: First, husband and wife often both work, while they have young children, when they don't need to do so. They spend their money on new cars, color TVs in each room, campers, boats, and other nonessentials, all purchased so that they will be able to fulfill their own wishes. They don't usually take time to become involved in the Church because they are so busy with a lifestyle that means running in and out of the home, fixing TV dinners, going out with friends several times a week, providing almost "live-in" babysitters, sitting in front of the boob tube when they are home, and so forth.

Not at all surprising is the communication pattern developed in this type of family. More often than not husband yells at wife and wife at husband because "You didn't fulfill my needs!" These emotional outbursts are not limited to the husband and wife alone. Parents will treat their children with the same harsh words and then punish them when they parrot their parents' behavior as they interact quarrelsomely with each other. The entire family then becomes entrapped in a downward spiral that eventually causes disintegration of the family unit.

A perfect example of this imperfection was observed by a friend of ours at a shopping mall:

66 "My family and I had just got out of our car and were walking toward the mall entrance when we saw a very well-dressed man and woman standing by the open trunk of their new Cadillac. We stopped, uncomfortable and embarrassed, when the man began pushing his crying, infant son down into the trunk so that he could close the lid. The lady, seeing the resistance of the boy, stepped over and slammed the child in the back with her fist. It was at this point that we were noticed. The man grabbed the son, yelled at his wife about making a scene, threw the boy into the back seat of the car, motioned for his wife to get in, and quickly drove off. I had never experienced child abuse before, and I spent the rest of the day crying about it." **99**

Can you imagine how saddened our Heavenly Father becomes when we treat each other in such an unloving and uncaring way? Lest we create an imbalanced perspective, thinking only of sins of commission, let us share another experience with you:

66 "One of my best friends in high school was always thinking of others. Now, it has long been a tradition at Springville High School to place the names of those students having birthdays during the month on a calendar which was displayed at the front office. My friend, as he was going to class happened to glance at the calendar. He felt badly when he noticed that Bill, a friend of his, had a birthday just two days before. Later in the day when my friend saw Bill, he motioned him over and said, 'I saw that I missed your birthday the other day, and so I just wanted to say Happy Birthday!'

"It was then that Bill responded in a bitter tone, 'It doesn't matter. My family didn't remember either.' " **99**

Perhaps the saddest thing we have observed about the lack of caring is that it is a sin. As such, it must ultimately be repented of, and like most other things, such repentance can be extremely difficult.

66   "Well, it's been two years now and it still bothers me. I guess I should expect this feeling around Christmastime, but I don't think I'll ever get used to it. If I had only returned half the love that Danny shared with me, I probably wouldn't have the guilt complex I own even today as a junior in college.

"I can still remember the day that Mom brought Danny home from the hospital as a newly born baby. I was only four years old at the time, but it felt kind of nice having an additional member of the family around the house; especially a baby brother. Everything seemed normal to me; the dirty diapers, empty baby bottles, baby powder smell and the crying at irregularly spaced intervals, especially at night.

"Yet, something wasn't quite right. Mom and Dad's incessant nightly discussions, which I interpreted as well as a six-year-old could, concerning Danny's development, confirmed what little I understood. Danny was what my parents called 'partially retarded.'

"Mom continually referred to Danny as being 'special,' which began to bother me. Wasn't I 'special,' to anyone anymore? How come I didn't get any special attention? What originated as an inconspicuous dislike soon developed into a totally visible resentment of Danny. Such a relationship would only be more complicated by the fact that sooner or later, Mom would expect me to look out for Danny because of his special problem. Not if I could help it!

"When it finally happened, this long-awaited occasion was temporarily, if not cleverly, postponed when a quick-minded, fleet-footed maneuver left Danny far behind in a bundle of tears. After an hour or so of fun with my friends, I headed home only to find Danny sitting in the exact spot where I had abruptly abandoned him. As I approached him, a large smile beamed despite his tear-stained eyes and runny nose.

"He helplessly hugged my arm and murmured my name thankfully. I proceeded to take Danny home, consumed with the fear of what my parents might do when Danny explained what I had done.

"Much to my amazement, Danny never mentioned a word. In fact, that night he came to my room and thanked me for helping him when he was lost.

"That was not the last time I would betray Danny's trust.

Whenever I took Danny to play with my friends, he immediately became the focal point of vicious name-calling, which was usually instigated by myself. I never missed an opportunity to entertain my friends by either verbally or physically shredding Danny's world.

"This treatment continued right into my high school years, until I just completely avoided any sort of interaction with him. It wasn't so much that I resented Danny's favored treatment anymore as it was that I just hated to be seen with him for fear of what would happen to my image. Then, after my acceptance to college, I no longer had to worry about Danny's little feet clumsily pounding the pavement behind me.

"Mom occasionally wrote to me, telling of how Danny would sometimes cry for hours concerning his big brother's absence. She mentioned that the only consolation for Danny was that his big brother was coming home for Christmas in two weeks.

"Danny had been saving his money for over two years in order to buy a bike which he had seen some time ago in a store window. This would be the Christmas that he would be able to afford the purchase of it with his own savings. Danny was now thirteen and Mom had gotten him a paper route which enabled him to save a little money. He really was a hard worker and a real saver when it came to money.

"One day when Mom returned from work, she found a small butter knife along with Danny's empty piggy bank sitting in the middle of his bedroom rug. She pondered the situation until it finally dawned on her. Danny had been on the extension when she had phoned me at college to find out what I might like for Christmas. I had mentioned that I might like a nice camera.

"Mom's hunch was confirmed when Danny arrived home late for supper with a large brown paper bag in his arms. It was covered with Hampstead's Camera Shop advertising written all over it. Danny tried to hide it, but Mom hugged him before he could get by her. Danny knew that Mom understood.

"The day had come for me to return home for Christmas, and I was happy to have done so well in my first semester at college. The bus trip home was about a five-hour ordeal, but some good reading and some reminiscing could be done. Home would be fun just for a change and I suppose I could even put up with Danny for ten days. Little did I know what awaited me at home. When the bus finally pulled into the station, it was snowing lightly and the night lights shone brilliantly as they reflected off the powdery white blanket. Home was only four blocks from the bus station and the walk would be especially nice for collecting my thoughts. When I got within sight of the house, I thought to myself what a welcome sight it was.

"How wrong I was.

"When I entered the house I heard Mom's soft quiet voice. I followed the angelical voice to Danny's room and, pushing the door ajar, found Mom partially cradling Danny in her arms beside his bed, her voice intermittently broken by sobs.

"Dad gently escorted me to the living room as he sensed an explanation was due. It seems that Danny, while on his paper route, had passed Sluice Pond at the same moment a young man had carelessly fallen through the thin ice. Unhesitatingly he rushed to the young man's aid only to find himself in the very same predicament. Both were saved by three older passersby, but not before Danny had become unconscious. It was several hours before he regained total consciousness, but he had also contracted a deadly case of pneumonia. His breathing had become erratic due to congestion and several other complications.

"Christmas eve came and Danny grew worse. That night Mom told me that Danny wished to see me. When I approached his bedside, he immediately clenched my arm with his hands. Mom, on cue, entered the room with a wrapped package and handed it to me. I read the card attached: 'To my big brother who I love a lot. From Danny.'

"I opened the package and Danny smiled. Then he asked if I had a present for him. I really hadn't but I said that I did. I said it was so big that I had to leave it at the bus station and it would be delivered tomorrow.

"I hurried quickly out of the room with tears in my eyes and hopes of catching the store open where Danny's long awaited bicycle hung. What luck! The store was still open and I made the purchase. I carried the bike home and placed it in front of the tree, attaching a small card: 'To my little brother who I love a lot. From David.'

"All to no avail. Danny never saw his present from me. He died that night in his sleep.

"He never heard me say, 'Danny, I love you,' because I was always too busy, stingily taking all that he offered me. Well, it might seem foolish, but I'd just like to say it now: 'Danny, wherever you are, I love you very much.' "

As you read, did you note the different examples of noncaring mentioned by the boy? Most obvious, of course, was his unconcern for his younger brother. But it was also obvious that when he was a youngster his parents had become so engrossed in Danny's problems that they somehow forgot for a time—a most crucial time—that the older brother had needs, wants, and feelings also.

It isn't very difficult at all to focus on obvious problems to the exclusion of less visible ones. In our classes we find ourselves over and over giving 90 percent of our attention to the 5 percent of the kids who have the most visible problems. It is normal, but it isn't very fair to the others, the "good kids" who seem to need so little help and attention.

Moms and dads, sons and daughters, brothers and sisters, please remember that we were all placed in families so we could help each other in an atmosphere of love based on total knowledge of each other. This knowledge, this understanding, this love must be built up a little at a time, much as we would build up a stone fence. We gather the rocks together, mix the mortar, and build it up one stone at a time with good mortar to hold it all in place. In the same way, as we add mortar to the walls of our families, it would be well to keep in mind that the consistency of the mud is crucial. If we water down and dilute the relationships we have by not caring, then our walls will eventually crumble to dust. However, by caring and concerning ourselves with each member of the family we can be constant in our love and thus develop a consistency which will give strength as we build eternal homes in which to live and experience joy.

Now let's look at some experiences of families who genuinely care for each other.

" "My littler sister, Sandi, who is now nine years old, is one that always reacts positively to love and attention directed her way. Being nine years younger than me, she relishes any attention that her big sister gives to her; therefore any act of sharing has great importance to her.

"For example, last Christmas she had a minor role in a play that the Primary was putting on, but it was a major event in her life. When she found out that the rest of the family had other plans and would not be able to be there she was mentally crushed at the idea of no support. I could see that the dilemma, in her eyes, would seem like the end of the world, so I told her that for part of my date we would make sure that we were at the church in order to see her little play.

"She was so overwhelmed and astonished (if a little girl can be all that!) that she nearly cried in pure delight. She did very well and informed everyone that her sister had come 'just to see her!'

"This taught me the valuable lesson that giving a few minutes to a person can mean the world to them and effect an eternal relationship of love and caring." **"**

Another example:

" "Leaving school for the Thanksgiving holiday seemed like an 'it will never arrive' dream. My freshman year at the Y was moving rapidly, but being away from home for my first time was not the easy adjustment I had anticipated it to be.

"Thanksgiving Day arrived for me as I awakened to a small shaft of light through the break in my bedroom curtains. It was a day I will always remember as we indulged in Mom's special homemade rolls, my favorite dressing, and finally the pumpkin pie.

"By Friday things seemed back to normal; normal in that my sister and I were once again finding picky little things to fight about. You see, my little sister Wendy is three years younger than me, and very attractive. She has always seemed more my age. Perhaps it was because of this that we resented each other at times, and thus developed distance in our relationship. In looking back it is now apparent that the only times we acted as if we cared about each other were on birthdays and at Christmastime, and then only because it was expected.

"It was while washing up the evening dishes that I first noticed my sniffle. It wasn't even an hour later that I resigned myself to a good old-fashioned head cold. Saying good night to my folks and making one final sweep to the Kleenex box, I headed for bed.

"Upon reaching my room, I discovered once again the draft on the floor as I hurriedly said my prayers. Climbing into bed I recall begrudging Dad's constant vigil with the thermostat. Energy conscious—too energy conscious, I thought. Now, for the first time, I noticed that one of my blankets had been removed from my bed—undoubtedly taken by Wendy upon my departure for school.

"The hours passed slowly as I tossed and turned, consuming what seemed like an entire box of Kleenex. Several times I considered getting up to hunt down my second blanket, but somehow the strength was just not there.

"Shortly after two in the morning I heard my door being softly opened. In the dark I saw the shadow of my uncaring younger sister. I started to wonder what she wanted this time, but was cut short in my thoughts as she softly and gently covered me with another blanket and tucked me in snugly. Without a word she tiptoed from the room, leaving me with tears in my eyes and wonder in my heart at her tender love so beautifully and secretly shown." **"**

There's something about caring that makes you feel good in spite of yourself!

" "Tired and cold, I bumped the mud from my shoes. It had been a successful hunt, with the dove season beginning only this morning. 'Gee, it's great to finally be sixteen,' I thought to myself as we crammed ourselves in the cab of Dad's truck.

" 'Hey, you guys,' I said, 'I'm starved! Let's head on over to the malt shop before we go home.' With a chorus of agreement, I shoved the truck into second and away we went.

"We ordered our soft drinks to go, and were just leaving the parking lot when a yellow jacket hornet flew into the cab. Although the other guys saw it, they conveniently failed to warn me, as it landed on the inside edge of my cup. They held their breath as I took my next drink. As luck would have it, the hornet turned as the cup came to my lips, and in one fell swoop, its needle-like stinger plunged into the center of my upper lip. Within three seconds their laughs turned to moans as my malt landed all over their laps. This eased the pain only for a moment, as my lip began to swell and throb.

"By the time I got home the pain was excruciating. I began to feel nauseous and so without a word to the folks I headed for bed. I hadn't been there for more than a couple of minutes when Mom and Dad both came in to see what was wrong.

"The hours passed slowly, and with a great deal of pain. But more than the pain I remember that Dad came in and checked on me every two hours throughout the entire night.

"Here I was sixteen years old, and Dad cared enough for me to demonstrate his concern in such an unselfish way." **"**

For the past few pages, we have experienced many caring moments in families, as seen through the eyes of young people. Let us now journey into the home of a very special friend.

In this home we find a large family, a family blessed with an unusually choice son and brother. While only sixteen years of age, Steve has gained a maturity and sense of purpose that many people live an entire lifetime without obtaining.

You see, as a young boy Steve began to lose his seemingly endless strength. It was not long before the doctors diagnosed his illness as terminal muscular dystrophy.

Giving Steve only a short time to live, they did not take into account that Steve was to serve a very special role in his family: he would become the cement which would glue his family into a celestial unit.

Today, almost ten years later, Steve motors around in his electric wheelchair, too weak to do anything but push the button, and yet strong enough to give strength to each member of his family, as well as to all of those whose lives he enriches, as his mother explains:

66 "Life is so fragile. Before we learn this, relationships can be less meaningful than they should be. As I reflect back through our nineteen years of marriage, I can see where the change began for us. The first years of our marriage were fun and carefree, and yet as life became more complicated it also became more meaningful.

"The summer our son Steven went through a series of tests was the real beginning. It took years for the facts to really sink in for all of us. Little by little as Steven's body became more frail and weak, we realized more and more what caring really implied. He helped to teach us how important it is to make the best use of time with each other. Before we lose him to this life, we must give and take as much love as we can, so both he and we will be able to live on that and remember until we are reunited in the life after this.

"Steven's cheerful attitude and ready smile for his family warms our hearts and we are so grateful for the impact he has on our lives. We no longer pray for him to be well and strong and to have a long life, although for a long time we wanted that and prayed for it. Steven, too, no longer asks for that. He is aware of our Heavenly Father's desire, and by knowing his role he accepts it fully. This acceptance has again and again warmed our hearts and has kindled a flame of caring and love deep within that cannot be described with words." **99**

Let us now continue to gain insight into caring by listening to the words of Steve's older brother, age seventeen:

66 "I truly believe having Steve in the family has helped us to care more about each other. We all have to give in to Steve a little, which in turn makes it seem more natural to give in to each other. This is, I believe, a huge chunk of the caring parcel.

"It seems that as time passes we do more and more things as a family unit. The result of spending so much time together is that we have learned what it means to be patient with one another. We have found that Steve requires help which, if everyone isn't happy, will make us angry and impatient with each other. As a family we try to steer away from that. Anger is a tool of Satan; it is something that comes quickly and yet is hard to drive away. We now realize that practicing patience develops patience because it is a hard thing to keep within ourselves. We work on patience a lot as a family, and that may in fact be the place where the most sacrifice comes from.

"One of the greatest blessings I have had as Steve's brother is to receive of the strength that he offers. He is so determined in life and so compassionate with others that at times it makes me feel like shedding a few tears. If Steve could walk perhaps we would not be the family that we are; and so, beginning with Steve, we are all grateful for things just the way they are." **"**

One of the most profound lessons we can learn in life is the value of sharing our innermost feelings with each other. For some, openly sharing and expressing care and concern may be difficult. But such a difficulty is not insurmountable. As we (the authors) grew up together, our parents taught us by example that what you really want to do, you can do. Father once typed on a card that Mother then taped on the refrigerator at our eye-level: "That which we persist in doing becomes easier to do; not that the nature of the thing has changed, but that our power to do has increased."

If giving seems hard to you, then the way to make it easier is to give as much and as often as you can, until the act of giving seems natural. If cheerfulness does not come easily, then act as if you are cheerful for several days and you will surprise yourself to discover that you really *do* feel pretty good!

We become what we expect ourselves to become; we do what we expect ourselves to do. And by acting as if we were the kind of person we want to be, we make it easier and easier to actually *be* that kind of person.

So far we have primarily given examples of caring by parents for children or caring by brothers and sisters for each other. As our parents grow so old that they are no longer able to care completely for all their own needs, we have a rare and perfect opportunity to repay great kindness and love and concern from the past. As our parents were able to give us love and security without stifling our independence, we are able to give to them in their time of greatest need the same choice gifts.

We as brothers reflect with fondness upon our opportunity to have our grandmother live with us as we were growing up. She moved from home to home, so that each of her children could have that blessing and added spiritual dimension in their home. It was such a treat to help her with her suitcase and rocking chair, as those were the two essentials which traveled with her. Although she wasn't able to kneel, we will always treasure the times we knelt around her in that rocker, teased her a bit, and then had our family prayers.

Leaving our own experience, we would like to share the reflections of a friend:

66 "My great-grandmother was a great pioneer and child of God. She bore and reared ten children who were close to the gospel of Jesus Christ. Being the wife of a rancher and stockman, her life in central Utah was anything but easy. She died in 1966 at the age of ninety-five. Although her mind remained clear and alert, her last twenty years on this earth were years of misery. This was due to her physical ailments, as she was nearly blind and suffered from other problems such as ulcers and varicose veins.

"During this dear lady's final three years my grandparents never left her side. They insisted upon sacrificing their own comforts to tend to her every need. They did this, even though the rest of her children wanted to either put her in a rest home or hire someone to take care of her. My grandfather would lift her and carry her to the bathroom and other places. And so it was not a surprise that she reached the point when she would not let any of her sons carry her, but only my grandfather, her son-in-law, in whom she completely trusted.

"It was soon after this wonderful woman died that another great-grandmother needed these two unusual people. She had also given birth to and reared a large family under adverse conditions. She died in 1974 at the age of ninety. Most of her problems were mental rather than physical. She became quite senile during her last period on earth and once again my grandparents supplied her with constant care.

"It was interesting to me that once again the rest of her children wanted outside help to take care of her, but my grandparents felt a desire and an obligation to care for this lady.

"Even though my grandparents had children and grandchildren to worry about and love, still they spent ten years of their lives devoting constant care to their mothers."   **99**

Just an idea: As you read of these experiences with elderly relatives you probably formed in your mind a mental image of such an experience with your own parents or grandparents. As you did, is it possible that you also considered just your own feelings? As you contemplated doing a service for someone, bearing the burden, might you have been patting yourself on the back for a job well done?

Isn't it amazing how easy it is to fall into the trap of caring for the wrong reasons? If we truly cared, we would be performing this act of love with the objective of increasing the joy of our elderly loved ones, while in every way possible lightening their personal burdens.

This idea first came to Brent as he labored as a missionary several years ago in the Florida area. St. Petersburg was a city of the "newly wed and nearly dead" as his companion introduced it. That is, those living there were mostly retired people, usually without loved ones nearby, who marry for the fourth or fifth time, just to find happiness and to have their personal emotional needs fulfilled despite their age. It was not uncommon to see couples in their eighties and nineties holding hands in the park as they planned for perhaps a year or two of life together.

"Until then, I had never considered older people as having feelings and needs and desires," Brent recalls. "Yet, of course, they do, and all of us need to be aware of them as we interact with these special people who are struggling to 'endure to the end.' "

Heavenly Father blesses us with insights and personal revelation in various ways. We do not have to see a burning bush to feel his presence; we have only to open our spiritual eyes to each of life's experiences.

Whether we are struggling to free ourselves from the binding ropes of not caring in our family relationships, or whether we are free to lift up and serve others, it is exciting as well as comforting to know that direction in caring is given as we are "in tune" to receive. Heavenly Father cares how well we care, and is willing to teach us.

A few years ago Brent prepared a seminary lesson in which he placed a world globe on the desk in front of the classroom. He then darkened the room as the students entered, so that they could not tell that anything was sitting on the desk. Neither did the students know that in the rear of the room was a spotlight—turned on, but covered so the light wouldn't project.

He had aimed the potential light upon the globe on the desk, and as he gradually uncovered the light, more and more of the globe was revealed until at last the whole world was identifiable. By the time the spotlight was completely uncovered, every detail on the globe could be examined.

He then asked the students to express their insight into what had just happened. Almost immediately it was apparent that they were seeing an analogy to the way our Heavenly Father, after his children had insisted on wandering in darkness for so long, finally released the light and warmth of his Holy Spirit upon the earth. Brent then explained how this resulted in the insights and successes of Luther, Calvin, Wesley, Smith, and many others which, of course, eventually led to the restoration of the fulness of the gospel, a process still going on today.

We grow in an understanding of our Savior's teachings "line upon line, and precept on precept," just as the students' vision of the globe improved as the light gradually illuminated it. Each day we become more and more enlightened as we take upon us this mantle of Christ. Each day we learn better how to care for others in righteous ways as we are prompted by the Holy Ghost.

5

FRIENDS FOREVER

66 "A few years ago I had the opportunity of babysitting a neighbor
boy up the street from where I lived.

"Bobby wasn't like everyone else I tended. He was severely
mentally retarded. Bobby's parents had known before he was born
that something wouldn't be quite right, and they had knelt and
prayed prior to delivery for strength to accept and love their new
child.

"The years passed, and when I began to tend Bobby, he was
sixteen years of age—the same age as myself. Although a teenager,
Bobby was only the size of a four-year-old. In addition, he was so
retarded that he was almost a vegetable. Not being able to speak, he
could make no requests, and thus could do nothing for himself. He
would open his mouth very wide and a small squeak would come out
when he was unhappy. Bobby's parents were so good to him that
they hardly left his side. The doctors felt that he would live only a
few years, but due to the tremendous love from his parents, he lived
until age seventeen.

"Each Christmas his parents would ask me to babysit while
they would go to a few Christmas parties. When I first saw Bobby I
was shocked by his grossly misshapen body. Then came my moment
of truth. Bobby's mother sat me in the rocker and placed Bobby in
my arms. There we were, both age sixteen, and I had to literally grit
my teeth to even gather the strength to look at him.

"His mother told me that he liked to be held, and so there we
were—for several hours. I was really afraid to touch him at first, but
as I got to know Bobby, I realized that he had feelings just like me. I
became aware of what it was really like to learn to care for and love
someone for what they were inside, and not for what they could do
for me.

47

"One particular time I will never forget: I was holding him, rocking him, and trying to get him to stop his soft 'weeping' as he saw his mother leave the house. I finally got his attention and he recognized me for the first time. Bobby looked up at me and actually smiled! That little smile was the most special smile I had ever received in my life. That moment will forever linger in my mind, as from it I learned a most treasured lesson: When you really care about someone the smallest gesture of love means the most. A person doesn't need to give costly presents to show someone they care.

"It was almost a year later that Bobby contracted pneumonia and died. At the funeral a member of my ward approached Bobby's mother and said, 'It's a blessing that Bobby has passed on. It will be such a relief for you.'

"I was next in line, and as Bobby's mother saw me we both rushed into each others arms. As tears streamed down her face she said, 'Karen, *we* understand how difficult it is when someone you love dies.'

"I knew exactly what she meant. I wish everyone could have the experience of a Bobby in their life, for it is through sacrificing part of oneself that we realize the true perspective of life." **"**

Many young people grow old in a shell. They never experience the fulfillment that comes from caring. They spend their time developing me-itis—an illness that comes from being concerned only with themselves. Their entire orientation is toward getting and taking. As seminary teachers both of us repeatedly observe classical examples of this illness. Yet many young people have caring experiences that cure the disease and replace it with love and compassion.

One of the ways young people have of developing caring relationships is through dating. Dating is fun and exciting, but it is much, much more than that. It is a unique way to receive personal growth and development, as well as a special way to assist others in developing also. This is crucial, especially if you desire to one day begin dating in order to select an eternal marriage partner. We have known a few misguided (and lonely!) souls who felt that dating was unnecessary and that they could merely wait for the "right one" to come along and then get their hooks in, but good! And then there are others who date only for selfish reasons.

If we could pour one essential thimble-full of knowledge into your minds, it would be this: Your actions will greatly determine how the people you associate with live *their* lives. And vice-versa. A lot of young people doubt they have much influence on members of the opposite sex. They're wrong! Take this young man's account of a girl who influenced him:

66 "I have a girlfriend that I really think a lot of. She and her parents are not members of the Church. Being around them as much as I am has surely helped me to appreciate the Church and the things it does for me. My friend's parents won't let her join the Church, and so I'm thankful that she can live the gospel principles without being baptized. Lately, I've thought more about the Church than I usually do and my testimony is getting stronger because of it. I'm proud to be a member.

"I'm thankful for girls who always set the best example, both in their dress and in the way they act. If all the girls were like that, all the guys would respect their priesthood more and gain a stronger testimony. Thank goodness there are still girls like that around." **99**

Now listen to the words of a young lady as she shares her feelings toward her boyfriend and their relationship:

66 "My boyfriend, Clay, played football for the university he attends. Not too long after the beginning of the football season last year he was severely injured in one of the games. It was questionable whether or not he would be able to walk normally again, let alone be able to play football.

"Anyway, to make a very long story shorter, he was operated on and during the following two months was forced to make adjustments in his life that were very difficult for him.

"But during that time I felt more needed than I had in a long, long time. We both grew to depend on each other for support in many different ways. Mostly, Clay needed the caring and understanding that every woman seems to be born with. I fasted and prayed for him more sincerely than ever before. During that time when Clay needed me to share myself with him so much, I grew emotionally and spiritually so drastically that when I look back on it now I am even more surprised at the development that took place in my life. I was needed and was able to come out of my own self to care for someone and help him in his greatest hour of need!" **99**

And now an experience of a young lady whose father is presently serving as a stake president. Obviously, the environment in her home was healthy, for she became this type of person:

66   "About three years ago I met a boy who was about two and a half years older than me, and who had already graduated from high school. At that time I was a sixteen-year-old sophomore. I had previously heard of this boy before meeting him, and I knew that he had some bad habits concerning the Word of Wisdom, and that neither he nor his family were strong in the Church. I knew that his father was not even a member of the Church, and that as a result this young man rarely attended his Church meetings.

"I really grew to like this boy, as I had seen him around and talked to him a couple of times. He was fascinating!

"After a week or so, he asked if I would like to go out to dinner with him. I really wanted to, but my parents had established the rule that while I was in high school, I could not go out with boys older than high school age. Well, I asked anyway, and for some reason my mother said I could go with him.

"I could tell when I went with this boy that he was a very special person. He knew about my family and he knew that we were all very strong in the Church. He also knew that if he did not go to church and live a righteous life I would not be able to go out with him and thus our relationship would probably come to a halt.

"As time went on he began going to church and trying so hard to correct his bad habits. My parents only let me go out with him three more times because they felt like they could not break the family rule, while at the same time allow me to interact on this basis.

"Each night I would ask Heavenly Father during my prayers to bless him that he might be able to realize the truthfulness of the gospel, and as a result become worthy to fulfill a mission. Sometimes when I would be talking to this boy about the Church I would say things that I didn't even know, and it was then that I began to appreciate the power of the Holy Ghost. I really feel that this experience is the foundation for the testimony which I eventually gained.

"Time passed, almost a year, and with its passing came new pressures and involvements. As a result, we would talk less and less. It may seem strange, but this made me happy, because I knew that he was relying less and less on me, and more and more on the Church. My prayers continued for him, especially asking Heavenly Father to help him see the value of a mission.

"Today, this boy's family is totally active. His dad is going to church, and with faith and the Lord's help I know that some day he will join and lead his family with the priesthood. This boy is now on a mission, and doing exceptionally well. I know that this would never have happened without the help of Heavenly Father. To this boy, to his family, and to me this is nothing short of a miracle!" **99**

Influence goes both ways—young men can also strongly influence young women. Here are some true stories of ways that righteous young men have been able to improve someone's life:

66 "Often we don't realize who really cares for us until they actually say or do something which makes a significant change in our lives. One such person is Jack. Jack is my girl-friend's steady, and he had come to town for the weekend. When the following event occurred I had met him but once, and I figured that he couldn't care less about me. I found out differently.

"That Saturday night Jack and his date went out, and my date took me to the movies. I found out later that Jack had my friend home and was home himself by midnight. My date and I arrived home about 1:30 A.M.

"Now would you believe that Jack found out what time I got in, and was actually concerned! I found out later that it is very important for Jack to prepare for the Sabbath with the right spirit, which is next to impossible when early Sunday morning is spent wondering whether or not your date is going to kiss you good-night. I had never thought of this as not keeping the Sabbath, or as a poor preparation for Sunday activities.

"Jack cared enough about me, a near stranger, to let me know his feelings. That Sunday in sacrament meeting I was sitting near Jack, listening to the prelude music. He caught my attention and leaned over and spoke to me. He kindly and gently told me his feelings on the matter and suggested I seriously think about it. He said my date would respect me more if I asked to be in by midnight on Saturday. He also mentioned that if my date was a faithful priesthood holder he would understand and perhaps adopt the rule as his own.

"By caring about me, Jack made me realize how important it is for me to live all of the commandments to the very best of my ability." **99**

Let us now share the experience of a young lady whose boy-friend dared to be a *friend*:

66 "I had a date to a twelve-stake fireside with a young man who had been trying for quite some time to get a date with me. It was with a great deal of reluctance that I accepted, although once the evening began I enjoyed myself and his company a great deal.

"Following the fireside we went to a root beer float party that was being given by a friend in the area. It was a party for the entire district in our ward, over which my date was the leader. We arrived at his party, acquired our root beer floats, and immediately he began to introduce me to his friends.

"Then it happened! Thrusting his float into my hand, while at the same instant telling me that he would be back in a minute, he darted out the door.

"So there I stood, holding two root beer floats! Do you have any idea how devastating it is to be an unfamiliar female holding two drinks at once? It seemed as though I stood there forever! I tried to make conversation with several people, but to say the least, I am not the most outgoing person among strangers.

"After waiting for what seemed to be hours, my date entered the door—with another girl! I could not believe this was happening to me. I watched him out of the corner of my eye, and it looked as if he took this girl over to a group of people, made some introductions, then left them. He walked back to me, took his float, and began eating as though nothing of any consequence had happened.

"I quickly debated in my mind as to whether I had a right to know what had just taken place. My frustration finally got the best of me, and so almost angrily I turned and demanded an explanation. I will never forget the look on his face as he turned and looked at me calmly, and matter-of-factly said, 'The one sheep just left the ninety and nine, and I needed to bring her back.'

"At that disclosure I felt like a selfish social midget! My date's calling in the Church was that of district leader, supervising these people. Never before had I seen anyone care so much about a calling.

"I later found out that this girl was having a real struggle in making friends and remaining active in the branch. Thus, when he saw her leave he cared enough to stop everything and leave to bring her back. I will always remember this example of caring and comprehending the worth of a soul." **99**

And now, consider the following relationship between a very special young couple:

66 "It isn't easy living with a cleft palate. Psychological things

52

occur in your mind, and no matter what other people may say to you, this little mental thing does something to the way you think about yourself, as well as your perception of what others think about you. Many times you think that others just simply do not care.

"While growing up I didn't communicate with my parents like I should have. I had an older sister who needed help and thus required a great deal of attention. As a result, I received virtually no attention at all. I developed the feeling that I was just someone who ate, slept, and worked in our home. I honestly felt like the family just didn't care about me or my problems.

"This is not all. The kids at my elementary school teased me and made fun of me continuously, calling me names that hurt to the core. When I was old enough to go to high school and date, I merely watched all of my friends going out while I stayed home. This all seemed to add up to the fact that nobody really cared about what was going on inside me. They just didn't care.

"In all of this, the thing which hurt the most was that it was not until my senior year that my parents even bothered to find out what was wrong. By then it was too late. I now knew that I was very inferior, and I lived in depression, looking down on myself. I did have several friends, but I was sure they didn't like to be around me because I was no fun to be with. I was always depressed.

"Not really caring, they didn't take the time to find out what was happening inside of me. I was literally being destroyed by my low self-image. My personality was forever being pushed back because I knew my handicap would cancel any personality I might display.

"Finally it happened. I met a boy who became very special to me. He overlooked this handicap of mine and took the time to notice me for what I really was.

"For some reason when people see someone who is handicapped they tend to pity them and feel sorry for them. They are very courteous. Well, this boy did just the opposite. He cared. He cared so much that he was very sensitive to my needs, and knew when I was feeling inferior.

"It was because of this that everytime I became depressed, he would get mad. Every time I put my hand up to cover my nose or mouth, he would remove it. He knew that I didn't like to meet people, and so he was constantly introducing me to others.

"He didn't do this to hurt me, but to help. He did it out of love. He noticed. He cared so much that he changed my whole life. Yes, it was hard and it was agonizing, but what I went through was worth it all.

"He changed my attitude toward life and towards myself. I owe him so much for just caring, and I know that he will be rewarded by our Heavenly Father for this Christlike deed. Now, today I find myself happy, in love with life, and beginning an eternity with one who is worthy of that blessing." **"**

As you think of this experience, consider if you would the actions of a very unusual young man from California. This young man was an outstanding athlete, multi-talented, handsome, and very well liked. He would, at different times, date various girls whom he felt did not have much self-confidence. He would usually date the girl until he believed she had built her confidence to the point that other boys would be wanting to ask her out. It may seem unusual, but the whole time he was completely sincere.

Not every man-woman friendship leads to marriage. But that doesn't make those relationships any less valuable.

" "On a warm, sunny September day, the silhouette of a young couple could be seen under the shade of a tree—not an uncommon sight for Brigham Young University. They laughed as they remembered old times, hoping that the thought of this being their last day together would be forgotten amidst the beauty of the day and the pleasure of one another's company. It seemed so ironic to them that all the time they had known each other in California they had never given the other a second thought. But now that they would be eight hundred miles apart, a sudden common interest began to grow and develop between them.

"The laughter died down as the young man assumed a very serious expression on his face, and then, almost apologizing, said, 'Well, maybe it's a good thing I'm leaving, after all.' The girl tried to understand his thoughts, but then, looking up, she asked in a puzzled voice, 'What do you mean?' He stared hard into her big brown eyes and said, 'I guess because I'm finding out that I could become very attached too easily and too fast.' He couldn't hide the quiver in his voice.

"For the first time, the young girl realized how much Don cared for her and, in return, how much she really loved and cared for him. There wasn't anything said that hadn't already been said by others before, and his expression was neither poetic nor eloquent, but it was a simple and sincere confession of the growing feelings he had been trying to suppress during the past few days that they had visited together.

"The girl smiled softly at him and their eyes seemed to communicate an inevitable feeling of oneness.

"During the next few months they grew close to each other through the letters and phone calls that they frequently exchanged. And occasionally a beautiful bouquet of flowers Don had sent enhanced the girl's room. She came to appreciate all the many wonderful qualities Don possessed that hadn't been as evident during their short visit, and she felt inside that her Father in heaven must love her very much to send such a special young man into her life.

"Finally the long-awaited day arrived when again they could spend some time together and catch up on the many precious moments they felt they had been so wrongly deprived of. They went places and did things together and spent many hours sharing their ideas and feelings and discussing the things that were important to them. They talked of marriage and raising an eternal family, and how wonderful it would be to be together forever and see their children grow strong and firm in the gospel. The many long years of pain and preparation, waiting for that one special person to come along, all seemed worth it now, and being apart for a short while longer did not seem so bad when the blessing of eternity together awaited them.

"On a cold, rainy December night, the silhouette of a young girl could be seen, kneeling by her bedside. With a heart full of gratitude she thanked her Heavenly Father for the many blessings that were hers and then, pausing, almost as if it were an afterthought, began to pour out the feelings and desires of her heart. She spoke of Don and her great love for him and wished ever so much that Heavenly Father would help her know if the things she desired were right.

"Humbly she asked him to bless her with a burning in her bosom and that feeling of peace and warmth that she had felt with Don several times before. But suddenly all warmth and peace left her soul and she was now acutely aware of the cold hardwood floor on which she knelt. Her thoughts wandered, and she seemed to almost forget the very purpose for which she was praying.

"She struggled within to feel that peaceful confirmation that comes with making a correct decision, but instead found it increasingly harder to concentrate on what she was doing. The only warmth she could feel was from the tears which were now making their way down her cheeks and onto the mattress beneath her. How could something that seemed so right be so wrong?

55

"Tears filled their eyes as once again the young couple said good-bye, knowing that this time it might possibly be their last visit. The girl wondered for a long while afterwards what purpose Heavenly Father had for both of them and why two people who loved and cared for each other so much could not be together. And then, one January evening, she happened to run across this poem:

Together

Perhaps we can be together there,
In that next place
Where bodies are so pure
They pass through planets—

Perhaps there,
Where the light that lighteth the sun
Is kept on all night every night,
And no one watches for morning
Holding the cold off with a candle—

There, perhaps,
Where pain is exchanged
For peace and a memory—

You and I can touch as we pass
And gather in the good of one another.
We can love and give
In whatever loving, giving ways
There finally are.

We still will wish
To be together then, I think.
Perhaps then we shall know how.
Perhaps, even, we shall know why
We cannot be together now.

(Carol Lynn Pearson, *The Growing Season*, Bookcraft, Inc., 1976. Copyright 1976 by Bookcraft, Inc. Used with permission.)

"Suddenly a warmth and peacefulness that she had not felt for a long time filled her soul, and somehow she knew that no matter what happened, everything would be all right." **"**

The "eternal triangle" doesn't have to be bitter—if people care enough.

" "Showing someone that you care is really so simple to do, but often the simplicity gets overcomplicated in delicate situations involving too many feelings. I have a friend—and the reason we still share that friendship is that he took the time to show that he cared.

"There were three of us involved: she and I both vying for his attention. We got it fairly equally until this open-triangle relationship progressed to a point where it was obvious that a decision had to be made. The previous months' foreshadowing should have been enough, but I was trying not to look.

"It was the first part of June and he still hadn't signed my high school yearbook. He said he wanted to take it home and I recorded in my diary that 'it must be something special.' It took him several days to return it; he wrote a lot of prose and I thought it might have something to do with that.

"My mom teased me once that he was using it as a way of 'dropping me' and the more it stuck in my mind the more I feared that it was inevitable. Like most defense mechanisms, my dominant reaction was to seek more foundation to reinforce that which I wanted so badly to believe. Others had said that hate was easier than hurt, and though I knew it well, I learned a better way.

"His full-page entry in my yearbook simply stated that he would always love me for what I was and that which we had shared together and had taught each other; that our friendship would never be forgotten. I read and blinked hard and knew what was to follow; he explained that he loved us both but in different ways.

"He did it so thoughtfully, so carefully, with such consideration that I could not hate him or even her. It really hurt, but the flames of a hurt like that extinguish faster than those of the hate I might have felt if he had been callous with my feelings. He's on a mission now and we're still writing, and the girl waiting for him is my friend—all because he cared enough." **"**

Love is a very deep and at times difficult-to-understand emotion. Rather than talk about love exclusively in romantic terms, we would like to mention a few of our feelings as love relates to physical involvement with a member of the opposite sex.

Loving involves trust and respect in a relationship, and exploiting that trust in order to take advantage of one's own body as well as that of the partner causes a couple to lose the trust and, consequently, the respect they once had for each other. When this occurs, the relationship is usually on its last leg. Someone once said that true caring and love is "not taking someone where they don't want to go." In other words, we don't demonstrate our love for a person by constantly imposing selfish physical demands upon our partner. We would like to now share with you a true account of a person who is the result of such a relationship.

66 "I was born out of wedlock, having been conceived in an effort on my mother's part to trap her boyfriend into marriage. I guess she felt she loved him and that by this means she could convince him to marry her.

"On the contrary, he was convinced that their relationship had been merely physical and should be discontinued, although he did assist with the hospital expenses.

"For the first few years of my life I had the blessing of maternal love which was later replaced rather inadequately with the attention of a grandmother, my mother having gone to work out of necessity to provide for our needs.

"Later, for reasons unknown to me, I was placed in one foster home after another and as time went on I developed an extreme hatred and distrust toward others. I was then placed for adoption because of the inability of my mother to care for me. Soon I became one of the most disturbed children at the agency.

"During this time another woman even more special in my life came along. Due to medical reasons she was unable to have any more children, though she had already been blessed with one daughter. Her desire to have a son was so great that she and her husband decided to adopt. Although the Children's Bureau tried to convince them that my case would soon necessitate institutional help, they decided to take upon themselves the awesome responsibility of adopting me as their own son.

"With love, patience, diligence, and the teachings of the Church, they helped me to overcome these obstacles and become the person I am today. Without their timely love and encouragement I would have developed into a criminal, but instead I am becoming a true follower of our Savior. I have been sealed to them in the house of the Lord for all eternity, and for their care and love I will be eternally indebted." **99**

Unfortunately, it is rare for one raised in such circumstances to reach the point where this young man is today. Indeed, the consequences in the life of a child of a relationship like the literal parents of this young man had are almost never considered by such couples.

In contrast, consider the following words of a young lady who grew in her relationships to the point that she was prepared to meet an eternal companion. It's refreshing to see how she was programming her mind so she would recognize "the one" when he entered the drama of her life.

66   "Throughout the years of my life, I have built up a reservoir, a reservoir of stored dreams, ideas, and love; a reservoir which I refer to now and then, reflecting upon a time yet to be.

"In my mind's eye I have watched him come and take me into his world, a world I complement, a world he loves, and together we make each other whole within the confines of this world. His happiness is my joy. I am his sustenance; he is my rock.

"I have often seen myself with child, smiling at him, knowing that for me the moment of birth will be the sweetest taste of god-like joy I will know. I've seen us depressed, watched us quarrel, and felt the burden of a thousand worries; then I've looked upon a man and a woman, kneeling in prayer as they renewed their love vows, and I have known with a spiritual surety that we would never be alone.

"Already I have seen a change, a growth within us both, and I have marveled over it. I've watched our love modulating into deep understanding and profound companionship, highlighted by a kind of consistent passion. I've seen us become one, as our lives intertwined for the joys of those spirits we love so dearly.

"I've sensed a new and wonderful satisfaction happen to us, a satisfaction soul-like in nature, the thoughts of which have thrilled. In my dreams the wrinkles are creasing my hand now, and we can't run through the frosted fields anymore, but nothing can deprive me of the warmth of his hand on mine. I can see him twisting the gold band around an old and withered finger, a gold circle, symbol of eternity, and I know, with a beautiful kind of reassurance, that we stand on the brink of eternity, unafraid.

"These are my most cherished thoughts. I am for him, whoever he may be, and he lives to love me. Ours will be a sacred union, sanctified by God, and this union will be the biggest steppingstone to the achievement of perfection we will ever take. How different from the world it all is when viewed through the window of the gospel of Christ. His way is fulfillment, and the beauty of this union of man and woman is that it is synonymous with it.

"Is it selfish for me to want to marry in respect to what it offers me? I think so, in a way, for it is all to my own personal advantage, and how many of us, when aware of the potential joys marriage gives can turn our backs to its experience?

"Time brings me closer and closer to this spiritual happening, and I patiently wait, hoping that now I am preparing for the role of wife and mother, knowing that I am saving every bit of loving I can give for him alone, and praying that I will be all I want to be to him as well as to God." **99**

The excitement of this young lady can really be felt! Time and events have changed since she penned her feelings. She is now happily married to that "man of her dreams" and is as enthused about life and love as before. Only now, with several years of marriage behind her, she understands the piercing depth of those words written so long ago.

There are other forms of love and caring as well:

66 "Our history class had decided in unison to visit the Mormon temple in Mesa, just a few miles away. The temple had just been renovated and was open to the touring public, and so we were all quite excited.

"After completing the tour, I headed for the nearest bench to sort out my feelings. I was frustrated, as I wanted more than anything to understand the purpose and worth of the temple. This building was extremely precious to some of my closest friends and I wanted to understand why. So there I sat, probably looking more dejected and confused than ever. It was then that my teacher, who was not a Mormon, saw me and in an instant was sitting next to me. He asked me what was wrong. I simply looked at him and said, 'I really wish I could understand about this temple. I just don't get it.'

"He looked at me, put his arm around me, and told me that it wouldn't be until I understood the purpose of the ordinances spoken of in the temple that I would understand its worth. He reminded me that it was not the building but the ordinances that take place in it which give it such great worth to its members.

"It was from that comment that I decided to take the missionary lessons so that I could learn more about the Mormons. Though my history teacher was not LDS, to this day I feel so grateful to him for caring enough about me to come over and talk. He saw I was feeling down and came over, and then he cared enough to really think and help me understand my feelings. Just from one teacher being perceptive and taking the time to care, am I now a member of the Lord's true church—and the happiest girl ever!" **99**

Not always do adults find it easy to care for young people.

Occasionally young people's actions seem so unpredictably foreign that they confuse and put off even the most well-meaning adult. Yet even so, many adults really try to go the extra mile in their relationships with youth. Come with us into the office of another seminary teacher as he relates one of the most difficult situations he has ever had to deal with.

66 "A few years ago when I taught in another seminary down the road and around the corner a ways, a beautiful little girl I'll call 'Gertrude' used to come into class. She sat kind of in the back, on the one side. Well, some kids came to me one day, and they asked me, 'Have you ever noticed that Gertrude. . . .' and then described a totally repulsive personal habit that I had certainly not noticed. They all felt that something should be done about it, but they didn't know exactly what to do.

"So the next day I watched her closely as she participated in discussion. But as she went to reading in her book, as she got involved in her reading she did indeed do exactly what they said she did, a habit guaranteed to make people want to keep their distance.

"So I figured, well, somebody has to do something. She was too sweet a little girl to let that be keeping her from having friends. So I walked back as the kids were leaving the classroom and said, 'Gertrude, can I see you in my office for a minute?'

"She came in looking scared to death. I said, 'I didn't call you in to scold you, or anything bad. I just called you in because I'm your friend and I care about you.'

"Well, she relaxed a bit, and I wondered what in the world my next move would be. Fools rush in where angels fear to tread; but I'd already rushed right in. So I just looked at her and described her habit and asked if she was aware she was doing it.

"You could see the water level rise, and tears came to her eyes as she shook her head no. She had been completely unconscious of it. She cried and cried and cried and cried, as though she would never get over the embarrassment. But afterwards we talked, and she resolved that she would pay attention and see if she could overcome her habit.

"Next day in class we were talking, and she participated, and as I gave them time for reading in the text she just kind of clasped her hands together tightly and started reading. I was watching her, (not staring, I hope), but as she got involved in reading she forgot for a moment, and she started but just in time she noticed it, slammed those hands together, looked up at me and just smiled, and I smiled back. She had to do that a couple of times, but that was about it.

61

"Now, it's kind of tough to do things like that. I thought perhaps she would hate me. She moved away from our school shortly after that, and to another state. I never heard any more about her, but a year or so later I was down at BYU and in June here came a letter. It was addressed to the seminary where I had been teaching previously, and had been forwarded until it had finally caught me. I opened it up, not knowing who it was from, and in it was a graduation announcement and an invitation to attend. Then on the one side she had written, 'Thanks—so much!'

"It wasn't pleasant to call her in and talk to her about her problem. But it was wonderful to see that she had overcome her habit and that she not only didn't consider me her enemy, but even much later was thankful that somebody dared to care." **"**

We survived our teen years, and having observed hundreds do the same, we have concluded that most young people at one time or another question whether their parents love them and are genuinely concerned about them. One of the reasons for this is that parents assume the dual role of guiding and disciplining as well as loving; yet despite their "interference" the love is still there and ultimately we must all realize that.

" "Involved in everything, that's me! My day usually began at 5:30 A.M. I would get up and get ready for my early morning seminary class. Then throughout the rest of the day, besides English, sociology, and other academic subjects, I was in the Missoula Youth Symphony and the a capella choir of my school, and was a varsity cheerleader and a member of a modern dance group. Needless to say, I was overwhelmed with involvement.

"I must say, in looking back, that it was always such a special feeling to have all my family at my concerts yelling the loudest bravos at the sound of the last note and to have them at the football and basketball games just to cheer me on.

"One incident in particular when my mother showed she really cared was one weekend when I was returning from an orchestra festival in Billings, Montana, which is about five hundred miles from Missoula. It was about 3:00 A.M. when I arrived home. The house was still and quiet but the porch and hall light were awaiting my safe return home. After I had told my parents I was home, brushed my teeth and said my prayers, I crawled into bed and felt a note under my pillow. It read:

" 'The house is all quiet at 5:30 A.M.
Our meals are all gooey with butter and jam.
Six at the table is surely not many.
Oh, how we miss our red-headed Anne.
Your mother's no poet and, boy, does she know it!
Anyway we did miss you very much and we're so glad you're home!
Love,
Mom and everybody else.' "

Sometimes it only takes something simple to remind us of how much our parents care.

"I am one of the luckiest BYU students alive because I have the opportunity of living at home while attending college. I'm even luckier because in my home my parents really love me and are supporting me with that love in my daily life.

"My college major is nursing. When that decision was made, I had no idea that in Nursing 206 I would have to leave Provo at 5:30 A.M. in order to arrive at the Salt Lake Primary Children's Medical Center by 7:00 A.M. for my clinical experience. This meant a lot of self-discipline in getting out of bed by at least 4:45 A.M. in order to be dressed, have a word of prayer, eat breakfast, and be off. I thought that was hard, just getting up so early, but actually driving to Salt Lake City during winter semester was a real trial of my faith.

"By the second week of driving back and forth from Salt Lake, my energy was decreasing while my fatigue was increasing. In the early morning hours when everyone else in the world was asleep, I was racing to get ready—running about eight minutes late. I knew that breakfast would have to be sacrificed for the few minutes of extra sleep I took. What a price to pay for extra sleep, a grumbly stomach till noon!

"As I ran up the stairs to grab a glass of orange juice and a slice of toast, I could smell some bacon being cooked. I entered the warm lighted kitchen and saw that my place at the table was set, with breakfast on my plate.

"Mom came into the kitchen behind me, gently put her arm around my shoulders, gave me a little squeeze, and said, 'Zina, I heard you get up late and knew you were not going to have time to prepare your own breakfast, so I wanted to surprise you with one, just to help you have a better day.'

"We sat down together and had a word of prayer. Mom offered it, asking Heavenly Father to especially bless me that I would travel without harm and be able to accomplish the goals I had set for myself.

"That morning I had the most delightful and refreshing breakfast. I then gathered my books together and got ready to leave. As I was going out the door Mom handed me my lunch and gave me a kiss on the cheek. 'I love you, Mom,' I said. 'I love you, too, dear,' she smiled.

"I drove to Salt Lake with those last words penetrating my soul." **"**

We are convinced that it is especially exciting for our Heavenly Father to observe young people caring about people other than those their own age. This is not easy to do, especially when their lives are as full and busy as they are today. Yet caring both for those who are older and those who are younger will bring about some of the most memorable rewards possible.

" "Seven girls about fourteen initiated a "Secret Grandmother" campaign around the neighborhood. The program's main purpose was to bring a little happiness into a few older ladies' lives.

"The names of the girls were unknown by the grandmothers. Everything was done in secret, and the girls were very careful not to reveal their identity. Over a seven-week period many nice things were done. One particular girl, who enjoyed poetry very much, chose first to give a card along with a small booklet of poems. The poems were about friendship and the happiness it brings.

"The second week the girl delivered a basket of fruit to the doorstep, ringing the bell and then running behind a bush. The grandmothers had been told about a neutral home in the neighborhood where, if they wished, they could leave things for their secret granddaughters. After the basket of fruit, the girl received a thank-you note, handwritten and in rhyme, from her secret grandmother.

"The third week passed and Easter was on its way. So for a gift the "granddaughter" made a hand-decorated egg, molded of sugar and delivered in secret. In return she was given a huge Easter basket filled with candy, and another card written in poetry.

"The fourth week rolled around and the girl sent a bouquet of lilacs accompanied by a card saying 'scent' with love. The fifth week a homemade apron was the surprise for the grandmother, and she said thank you with a beautiful box of stationery. The sixth week the gift was a bottle of perfume, the seventh it was homemade bread.

"Then the big day finally arrived when the grandmothers would find out who their granddaughters had been. At a big luncheon held by the parents they were introduced to each other. But the special thing was that after the seven weeks were up the friendship shared by this girl and her grandmother did not end. Each had become very aware of the other and her needs, and to this very day they continue doing nice things for each other.

"In answer to the question, 'What did this experience do for you?' the girl responded: 'It started out with me doing the sharing, but it turned out that I got the most. I found a forever friend, one whom I will always love and be close to.' " **99**

The following experience happened to a seminary student of Blaine's. It may sound a little far-fetched, and perhaps he would have been skeptical himself if the principal had not seen the accident and the class members had not seen the car afterwards.

66 "To some, this experience might sound impossible, ridiculous, or even like a lie. But what really matters is what I know is true, right?

"The story deals with my most prized possession, my car. One day, about a week ago, I took my car to school. The road was icy and slick, and I couldn't turn very well. I turned in to park in front of the school, but I didn't quite make it. I was not turned far enough in. Just when I had backed up to try it again, I saw a car coming. All I could do was watch helplessly as it hit me.

"One of my big problems lately had been swearing. I don't know why I was doing it so much. I guess I started because all the guys at work did it too. But in seminary I had talked with my teacher about it, and he told me that Heavenly Father would help me quit if I really wanted to badly enough.

"So anyway, this lady crashed into the side of my car so hard it knocked me clear out into the intersection. It was sickening to watch, but I controlled my hot temper, held onto the steering wheel with all my might, closed my eyes, and said over and over to myself, 'Don't cuss, don't cuss, don't cuss!'

"All of a sudden I heard another loud bang. I didn't know exactly what it was, but I thought, 'Oh, no, another car has hit me!'

"But when I saw what it was, I became very happy, especially when I found out that the lady's car didn't have a scratch.

"I found that the whole side of my car had been dented in by the other car, but by remembering my seminary lesson about not swearing, I know the Lord blessed me; and the pop I heard was the whole dent popping out to normal again, so that all I got on my vehicle was a scratch about three inches long down on the rocker panel. You could see where the dent had been by the crinkled paint. But the dent was no longer there. My car was as good as new.

"My testimony was greatly strengthened by this experience, especially in learning not to get upset at things too easily. And that the Lord will pay you more mind and heed if you will keep your cool, and not go around blowing up, or feeling like you could pulverize somebody if they looked at you the wrong way. From this I have received a whole different set of attitudes than I had before." **"**

Now we would like to relate a special experience Brent had as a youth:

It was springtime, along about the middle of April of my junior year of high school. Dad had taught us the value of work, and of sustaining ourselves. This I had done since the age of twelve. The junior prom was coming up, and I was struggling to scrape together the bucks to attend. The only money I had to my name was five dollars I had accumulated for tithing purposes, but had procrastinated paying. I will never forget that Sunday morning as I fought with myself over whether to let that be my money for the prom, or whether to take it to priesthood meeting with me. My conscience won out, although I can't say that I had the best attitude about taking it.

Following Sunday School I retired to my bedroom to contemplate my situation, as I was broke and with no foreseeable opportunity to make the money I needed. You see, I was in charge of the prom, and so I had no choice but to go. The other problem I had was that I didn't have a suit to wear. Without thinking too much about my problem, I decided to test the Lord and see what would happen.

Crawling down to my knees, I forced a prayer. I simply told the Lord that I felt I had to go because I was in charge, and that I needed his assistance. I had been off my knees for perhaps ten minutes when a good friend, Kent Peterson, called. He told me that he wasn't planning on attending the dance, and asked if I would like to wear his new suit and tie. I could hardly believe what I was hearing.

After visiting for a few moments the doorbell rang, so we said good-bye and I ran to the door. There in the doorway was a neighbor, Morris Brereton, who owned the orchard near our home.

He just stood there and grinned—as only he could do. Finally, after what seemed like an eternity, he said, "How would you like to make some money?"

Without thinking, I blurted, "I'm on. What's up?"

"Well, I've got to have that ditch over there cleaned out, and I figure it's worth payin' for just to get it done."

It was all I could do to keep from smiling, but I confidently set my wage: "I'll do it, but only for twenty dollars."

He smiled again, and then extended his hand. When the door closed I just fell on the couch and beamed. In less than a half hour after I had asked, the Lord had completely answered my prayers.

Two lessons were learned from this experience, although the tithing lesson was the only immediate one considered. It was several years later that I reflected back to that day, as it was the first real ray of light warming my mind to this truth: God is aware of our smallest request. He may not grant them the way we would at times desire, but he does know us as individuals, and is concerned for each of us.

6

LOVE THY NEIGHBOR

Everybody heard about the 1976 Teton Dam disaster in Idaho. Blaine was one of the victims. Here is his story:

I was relaxing in my hammock teaching my son how to mow our lawn that Saturday morning when my neighbor Bill Hansen called over and told me to get out my boat; the Teton Dam had broken. We both laughed, and my wife a little later called out to our son to hurry and get the lawn mowed because we were going to have a flood. And thus began the most unusual year of my life.

Our home, like all the homes in Sugar City and Wilford and most of the homes in Rexburg, was flooded that day in June 1976. Around our home we had five feet of water, which was more than some and nowhere near as much as others, and our home stayed on its foundation, which was a mixed blessing at best.

But the caring started very early the next morning, Sunday, when two of my seminary teacher friends, Jerry Jex and Kendall Jensen, appeared at the door of our little tent trailer where the eight of us had spent the night camping on the hill, and took our six children with them to their homes in Idaho Falls. That afternoon my wife's parents drove up from Utah and took the children home with them. They kept our baby and farmed out the others to various of our brothers and sisters, and there they lived for the next eight weeks, cared for as though they had been part of each of the families they stayed with. They had no clothing but what they had on, and so our families and their neighbors took care of that by either buying or gathering up all kinds of clothing for each of the children.

Later that Sunday morning I made my way through the mud and debris to our home and read the sign tacked to a dead tree in the middle of our front yard for us to report immediately all bodies we found, and then slowly and quite numbly walked through the mud-covered upstairs portion of our home. I would have gone downstairs too, but the water was still at ceiling level. And smell? There is no way that I can describe the awful smell; but although I can't describe it, neither will I ever forget it.

That afternoon a neighbor, Jerry Glenn, who was also flooded, came over and helped me rip out all our carpet on the main level so the floors would dry out without warping. Beyond that, though, I was too discouraged to do much.

The next morning, following a pretty rough night, I was standing in my driveway with my hands in my pockets all discouraged and wondering just where to start when Bill Hansen walked over. Bill is one of the finest men I have ever known, and he has more of the true spirit of the gospel about him in terms of caring about others than most people. But he walked over, kicked me where a person ought to be kicked now and then, and told me to get myself down into the basement and make a place for a pump hose. I guess I looked a little surprised, so without another word he jumped up on my porch and descended into our water-filled basement. He was back in a moment or two, shivering and telling me that things weren't half so bad down there as they looked.

A little later he and Lee Meikle, another neighbor, brought over a tractor and a huge pump, and while Lee and Bill worked to get the pump working I made my way down into my basement.

To say the least the water was cold and slimy, and when my feet had finally reached the basement floor the water was at my chin when I was holding my chin as high as I could. I could tell that much of the mud had settled, leaving a deposit of nearly two feet throughout the whole basement.

I made my way slowly through the family room and around the corner into our two oldest sons' room, and I knew right off they hadn't been keeping it as clean as we taught them to. For right ahead of me, floating at eye level, was a big dead fish. I gulped a little, thought about what I was wading through, and then very gently pushed it aside so I could proceed, doing my best to keep my mouth and nose above water.

Bill and Lee finally got the pump working, and a little later Jerry and Kendall were back, loaded with buckets, boots, and everything they could think of. When I asked what they were doing they just grinned and pushed their way past me and waded down into the basement where they went to work, manning the pump and throwing destroyed belongings out the window, including all

70

three thousand books in my library. I will never forget my feelings as Kendall handed me an axe and told me to begin chopping up our beautiful Early American couch so we could get it outside. I gulped and hesitated, but after the first swing, it got kind of fun.

For four days those two men came early and worked late, crawling and slipping around and in and under that slimy mud, thoroughly enjoying every minute of it in a tremendous effort to bolster my wife's and my own spirits. And oh, how they succeeded! giving my wife, Kathy, and me the courage to face the months and months of reconstruction lying ahead of us.

I remember at one point Kendall and I had both reached down through about fourteen inches of muck to try and rip up a strip of carpet. I let go, and as I did he gave a mighty heave, the carpet tore loose, and Kendall flew backward and completely vanished under that filthy goo. Jerry and I helped him up, and as he wiped the muck from his face he smiled and asked, "Do I have any on my teeth?" That's the kind of cheerful attitude they had.

Their wives came up and helped Kathy clean a room enough that we could begin sleeping in the house again, and one day a whole group of seminary teachers came and pitched in with the rest of us, hauling out bucketful after bucketful of mud and debris. Many others came and helped, and those that didn't were helping someone else.

Then my father and mother, my uncle Lyn and my brother-in-law Edward came and spent several days hauling out more mud, tearing down destroyed walls, lugging out mangled furniture and appliances, and so on. It was Ed who finally broke into our storage room, and by the time he did so the wheat and cereal had fermented, mixing with the stored sugar; You have never experienced such an odor, all mixed up with flood mud. Two or three times, in between trips to haul out ruined food, we had to haul out a nearly ruined Ed. But always he staggered back to continue his heroic efforts in that foul room.

Later my brother Brent and his friend Don made a special trip up to bring us a hot water heater, and still later Dad and Ed Kitch returned from Utah to re-do our wiring and install a furnace; I cannot begin to count all the hours and sacrifices that were made by others in behalf of our little family. It is very difficult to tell people, especially those not in your family, how very much you love and appreciate them for their love and care. But we do, as do the thousands of others who were flooded and who experienced the same kinds of blessings. We hope they know and understand.

Shortly after the flood, cleanup volunteers started coming in by busload; men, women, teenagers, farmers, doctors, mothers—all of them with shovels and buckets right down in the mud with the rest of us, seeming to enjoy every minute of it. All told, over fifty thousand people gave of themselves to ease the burden of those who were flooded. And they weren't all LDS. The United States government was there doing their best to help, the Red Cross was fabulous, a group of Mennonites kept whole crews busy for months helping people rebuild their homes and farms, and so on. Everybody seemed to care, and I suppose that was what made it such a valuable and yes, even pleasant, experience.

In Romans 13 Paul makes an interesting comment about the Savior's commandment to love our neighbor as we love ourselves. He says:

> Owe no man any thing, but to love one another: for he that loveth another hath fulfilled the law.
>
> For this, Thou shalt not commit adultery, Thou shalt not kill, Thou shalt not steal, Thou shalt not bear false witness, Thou shalt not covet; and if there be any other commandment, it is briefly comprehended in this saying, namely, Thou shalt love thy neighbour as thyself.
>
> Love worketh no ill to his neighbour: therefore love is the fulfilling of the law. (Rom. 13:8-10.)

Love fulfills or supersedes the intent of every other law. If all of us had perfect love for every other person, there would then be no need to have any other laws or commandments. Each of us would base his thoughts, actions and statements upon how they affected every other soul, and we would do, think, and say nothing that might be harmful to another. That is pure love, a love that is godlike.

You have no doubt noticed the bad things that go on daily in this world of ours. We read of them in the newspapers, hear of them on the radio, and watch them nightly on our televisions. Happily, that is not all the news. If it were we would live in a world where no one cared about anyone else.

But we don't, and all around us every day people just like us are exhibiting Christlike love by caring for and about other people in many many different ways. Sometimes the things done for others are gigantic in nature, but most often they are small and unnoticed—except, of course, by the ones involved. *They* always notice, and their lives are changed because of them.

72

The doer becomes more like the Master simply because he is doing what He would have done. The recipient becomes more like the Master because he begins to understand love a little bit better.

When someone cares, everyone is blessed.

" "My family was caught in a blizzard when Dad hit some black ice and skidded off the road into an abandoned pickup that was parked there. Dad died on the operating table.

"Mom and the kids who were with them, after a few operations, were in the hospital to regain their strength. From this nightmare we began to feel and understand the law of charity, the pure love of Christ. What a blessing it turned out to be.

"Strangers from Denver, the bishop and families from Church, came regularly. They called the part of the family who were not there and broke the news. They brought food and clothing to the kids. Our home teacher from Farmington, New Mexico, flew his plane to Denver, picked up the two boys when they were released, and flew them home. Flowers, cards, and people were always there.

"The Relief Society organized not only the sisters in the ward but Dad's school, the neighbors, and special friends so that each meal for two weeks straight was brought to us. Someone was always there to talk with.

"Mom came home about ten days later, finding friends, relatives and the Lord's Spirit to comfort her. All the funeral arrangements were taken care of and our home became a constant flow of people, either cooking or just loving her.

"The funeral was beautiful. Over a thousand people attended, over a hundred sang in the choir. All this strengthened each of us.

"After the funeral we found extra nice surprises. The town people got together and bought Mom a beautiful 1977 Impala, a car nicer than any we had ever owned before. Their explanation? 'Janice, you needed a car so we bought you one.' A scholarship fund was set up for the three kids at home. Mom was given a two-thousand-dollar scholarship to go back to school. The school superintendent offered her a job teaching if she went back to school and got her degree.

"Our home was leased, we rented a home in Orem, and off we went with a friend moving all our furniture and belongings in his van free of charge.

"Many other kind deeds were done, all of which if written would take hours. But the important thing is that it was done. People cared about us and did go beyond the ordinary.

"We as a family will never forget the lesson we learned, the restored love and confidence we experienced and now want to give to someone else." **"**

Often we are called upon to care about our neighbors during times of great personal tragedy. This is never an easy task, but it makes it a little easier when we understand that our mere presence can give great comfort, even though we say or do nothing else.

" "Erich Splettstoesser is a seventy-one-year-old rock of a man who has spent most of his life swimming against the tide of social discrimination and injustice. Born in what was once the East Prussian state of old Germany (now Kaliningrad, Russia), his life has been a collage of experiences ranging from playing the organ in the Lutheran Church to consulate work in Spain to smuggling refugees across the border from East Germany directly after the war. Never having married, Erich lived an exciting but lonely life.

"Elder Werner Madei and I made Erich's acquaintance in September 1976 at his home in Schwelm, Germany. Rapidly we became very close friends, spending many hours sharing feelings and experiences with one another as we taught him the gospel. More than almost anyone I have ever known he seemed to have a natural feeling for caring about people, and he did so despite the risks to himself. In November he shared with us an experience that I will long remember.

" 'On a night just like this in 1943, I was visiting a close friend in Berlin. It was one of those cold, clear October nights when you can count every star in the sky. Sitting on the veranda we spent a pleasant evening gazing into the heavens and chatting. I'll never forget how clear and bright the stars were that evening.

" 'Around 9:00 P.M. we began to hear airplanes in the distance. You could always tell when an attack was about to begin, for the sirens would sound, followed soon after by the *voom-voom-voom* rumbling of the planes' engines. Like a wave rolling across the land, the sound would reach a crescendo, die out, and then crescendo again, all the time growing in intensity.

" 'We ran out of the house and were outside when the first bombs began to fall. The target was a fuel supply depot about two hundred meters away from us. People began screaming and yelling from everywhere. All you could see were the exploding flashes of yellow and orange. Luckily they missed the depot, or I wouldn't be here telling you this today.

" 'There was no cover so I braced myself against a concrete pillar. Everything began to get dizzy, and I felt like I was slowly swinging from one side to the other. Then I realized that it wasn't me moving, but the pillar I was clinging to. With each explosion it would rock back and forth.

" 'Gradually the attack subsided. Chaos remained though after the bombers had gone. Everything was on fire and bodies lay everywhere. Some were dead, others dying. I ran to try and help a young girl who lay in the street in front of me. She was just seventeen and had both breasts blown off by an explosion. It was so sad, for she had just become a woman. She looked at me and just kind of sighed and was gone.

" 'Just to my right a Frenchman was screaming, "It hurts! It hurts!" He had been hit in the stomach by some flying shrapnel. I cradled his head in my lap and tried to comfort him some, and almost instantly he quit screaming and became quiet. Sometimes, just the assurance that someone is standing by will quiet and comfort a dying person. With that same sigh, he too died in my arms. It's almost like a last gasp, you know. They breath deeply, exhale, and then they are gone. Very peacefully.

" 'I've never felt so helpless in all my life. Up in the sky everything had been blacked out. There wasn't a star to be seen. It wasn't much, but that night I thanked God that maybe I had helped these two who had returned to him. I hope they are happy there.'

"That night as my companion and I drove home I thought of all the World War II books I had ever read. One particular book from the seventh grade stood out in my mind, *Airwar Against Hitler's Germany*. I remembered seeing the aerial photographs of recently bombed cities. It all seemed so mechanical and unreal back then. But it wasn't mechanical, it was all too real. That night I too learned a little about caring." **"**

Another example:

" "One act of caring that particularly touched my life was when our home burned down. I was in the fifth grade then and our family lived in the oldest house in Jerome.

"The house itself was beautiful; two stories with ornate carv-ings on the ceiling that divided the foyer, front room and dining room. The windows were old-fashioned cut iron and there were massive gold chandeliers in each room. A heavy polished wood stairway led to the upstairs foyer, which was hexagonal in shape, each wall branching off into a bedroom. I loved that house.

"Because it was so old it burned quickly. The fire started in the attic and in less than half an hour the top story had been completely destroyed.

"I had grown up believing that this was a dog-eat-dog world and that no one cared about anyone else. I had watched countless shows on television where violence was done to people and no one would come to their rescue. But when our home burned, my idea that people didn't care changed.

"Besides the firemen that fought valiantly to put out the blaze, twenty or so people ran in and retrieved furniture and our other belongings, all at their own risk. They continued to do so until all of our things were out, and by then the ceiling had given away. Many women ran to their homes and returned with old sheets and cloths to cover our furniture, protecting it from the winter weather.

"The kitchen was the last to go, and right before it did a man that we didn't even know ran in and all by himself carried out our refrigerator. Everyone was helping in one way or another.

"The ladies comforted Mother and immediately families volunteered their homes to us.

"The house was gone. Luckily it had been insured, but even with that the realization of what had been lost hit our entire family pretty hard.

"We rented an apartment, and for several weeks complete strangers brought food over. One woman even brought me a doll.

"Because of this experience I learned that most people are basically good and that they do care about others, especially in a time of need or emergency." **"**

And a simple thing that can make all the difference.:

" "A very special example of caring happened to me just a few days ago. I have been sort of sick lately, and one morning I fainted while in the shower. I had barely made it back to my room when a good friend came and knocked on my door. I usually never see her in the mornings and I can't imagine what made her come over that day. In fact, when I asked her later she said she didn't know why she had come. She just suddenly felt like she should come over and see me, so she did.

"I was very glad to see her. She made me get back into bed and then asked if she could do anything else to help me. It was so nice just to know that somebody cared, that someone was thinking about me and that I could ask her for help if I needed it.

"To me, caring is just all the little things a friend does, like knocking on your door to see how you are." **"**

Isn't that beautiful? Impressed by the Spirit, one woman does nothing more than tuck another into bed, and both have a beautiful experience with caring.

We don't have to wait for great tragedies to show we care, though when they come we certainly should do all we can to help. But caring involves just as much the little things as the big ones. Helping people with their daily problems as well as their major ones is perhaps the single most important concept of caring that we need to learn.

There are many times when caring is not easy. It is difficult to care enough about a person to tell him when he is wrong, either in his thinking or his actions, or when he has some personal problem or habit that needs to be changed. Yet if we care enough we will find a kind way to be honest.

And on the other hand, we will also be kind and receptive when someone who cares has the courage to be honest with us. That is fair, isn't it?

" "One of the most important events in my life, and one which changed my feelings about other people, occurred when I was a freshman in college. I didn't have a very good self-image, and this showed very clearly in my attitude toward others. I was living in the dorms and a couple of my friends lived down the hall from me. I found that I had very little patience with my roommate and my friends heard every little thing about it.

"Then one day for some reason it hit me. I don't know why, unless I was tired of feeling so awful, but I began analyzing myself and suddenly realized what I was doing. I would gripe at my roommate and then go find my friends and tell them all these crazy things and they would sympathize with me, and that would make me more angry than ever at my roommate.

"Anyway, my very good friend from home knocked at the door just when I needed a real friend the most, and he had the guts to tell me what I needed to be told and not exactly what I wanted to hear.

"He didn't give me any phoney talk about me just feeling sorry for myself and that stuff. He told me flat out that I was wrong in the way I was acting. And that is what a true friend does.

"He talked to me for a long time, and promised that he would help me. If he heard me yelling or griping at my roommate he would say, 'Watch it,' or something like that to let me know that I was slipping.

"He helped me a lot, and I find now that I am learning to love people other than those in my family, when I had never been able to do that before. I am learning to care for others, and I learned that other people really do care for me." **"**

In the book of Alma in the Book of Mormon a great deal of space and attention is given to Captain Moroni, a righteous military leader. In fact, he was so righteous that Mormon records that if all men would ever be like Moroni was, then the very powers of hell would be shaken forever. (Al. 48:17.)

But from what we are able to read, Mormon gives Moroni so much attention because he is using him to teach us the importance of freedom and the necessity of working to preserve it. Moroni's life was spent in this cause, and in the course of time he deals with draft evaders, conscientious objectors (real and fake), traitors, heroes, apparently non-supportive government leaders, and land-hungry enemies—in short, he dealt with almost exactly the same problems that we face today in attempting to preserve our freedoms.

Today we are under instructions to preserve freedom just as the Nephites were, and those instructions come not only from ancient scriptural instructions but also from modern priesthood authority. Loving our neighbor means that we will do our best to see that his freedom is preserved. And that can be done in many ways, including seeing to it that good men run for office, participating in elections, and being obedient to *all* the laws.

A friend of Blaine dreamed one night, and vividly so, that he was in his car and in a hurry to get somewhere. He was traveling about fifteen miles above the limit when a little child ran out in front of him. The child was killed and he was arrested, tried and convicted of involuntary manslaughter and sentenced to prison.

As the doors slammed shut behind him, he awoke. He later said that he had never in his whole life been so happy to find himself home in bed. And since that day he has never knowingly broken any traffic law. We all need to learn that lesson, caring for others enough to obey and support laws that protect them and their freedoms.

Certain occasions contain unusually good opportunities for caring, occasions when unless someone shows concern, a person feels most strongly the hurts and inadequacies in his life. Christmas is such a time. At that season more than any other we remember about our Savior and his perfect caring for us, when he gave the ultimate gifts of immortal life and freedom from the penalty for repented-of sins. So at the Christmas season we all probably do a little more about caring than we do the rest of the year, though this shouldn't necessarily be so.

Yet even at a season that promotes caring, some people go beyond the normal patterns to give a little more.

66   "I was in seminary just at the start of a new year. We were asked by our teacher to give a report on what had happened to us over the Christmas holidays. The kids began to relate the usual trips to grandparents' homes and the receiving of expensive gifts. But Kathy Humphries stood and told what her family had done for Christmas.

"At 7:00 A.M. on Christmas morning the children of the Humphries family hurried up the stairs and with explosive enthusiasm tore open their presents. After the initial excitement was over, and amidst all the wrapping paper, toys, candy, and clothes, their father gathered his family around him to have their Christmas family home morning. A prayer was said and then father inquired which present each of the children liked best.

"The family Bible was retrieved from the shelf and opened to Luke, chapter two, and the father read to his family Luke's account of the birth of Christ. After the reading there was a short discussion about the Savior's life. This went from his creation of the earth to his atonement. They then talked about the example of unselfish love which Christ had given us to follow.

"Next the father asked how his family, as a unit, could develop qualities similar to those discussed that the Savior exemplified in his life. The reply was to do unselfish acts of kindness to people they know.

"Marty Humphries, the youngest son, said he could start with a friend named Dave, who belonged to a very poor family. Dave seemed to be rejected at school. The father commented that that family was indeed poor, because their father had been out of work for some time.

"Then after a family brainstorming session the Humphries family unanimously decided how they could all begin developing a Christlike love. Fresh wrapping paper was brought out and each member of the family rewrapped his favorite present. Then they took down their Christmas tree and carried it out to their truck.

"By 10:00 A.M. the Humphries family was sharing Christmas

with another family, and both were enveloped in the happiness of the pure love of Christ." **99**

A married man shares another story of Christmas giving:

66 "This experience was one my wife had when a group of people shared their time, money, and Christmas holiday with her family.

"She was the next to the youngest in a family of nine children. Her oldest sister was married and she had two brothers who were serving missions at the time. The children at home ranged from seven to sixteen.

"Several months before, her father's leg had been crushed in a work accident. It was a very serious thing and he had been hospitalized for over three months. The family was, of course, having a hard time making ends meet because of the accident and because of the two sons who were on their missions. They had managed to survive, but the prospects of Christmas presents and other holiday finery were very dim.

"Her father was released from the hospital on the first of December, so the family was happy for that. He, however, felt very unhappy that he was unable to obtain things for his family for Christmas, and so as Christmas approached the holiday season was not a very pleasant one for him.

"His wife and the older kids did their best to make things as happy and cheerful as possible. They did have the Christmas spirit in their home, and they sang Christmas songs all the time, so everyone but my wife's father was cheerful.

"Well, on Christmas Eve there came a knocking on their door, and when they opened it there stood a typical big jolly Santa Claus. Some unknown persons had bought food and presents and had wrapped and fussed over every little thing as though they had been doing it all for their own family. The children were elated, the mother relieved, and the father a little embarrassed at the offerings but nevertheless very, very thankful and thrilled. The gifts were accepted graciously and my wife's family had a wonderful Christmas—it is the one they always remember now as they talk about their favorite Christmas.

"Some loving people had cared about them very much, and that is what made their Christmas so memorable." **99**

We would like to close this chapter by sharing with you the

experiences one family has had over the past five years as their neighbors and people in surrounding communities have cared enough to turn their personal tragedy into some eternally beneficial lessons on love.

The daughter of some good friends of ours was in an auto accident a few years ago and was paralyzed from the waist down. Almost immediately the caring began as friends and neighbors appeared, doing everything they could to help out. However, as time passed it became evident that their ordeal was not to be brief, but rather would involve years and years as well as take a great deal of money.

One evening as the family sat in council discussing where they could cut back financially, they heard a knock on their door. Their son went out, only to find a large garbage can on their porch. At first upset, they opened it to find it filled with hams, roasts, etc. Then clear at the bottom they found a coffee can; since they were Mormon, it was obviously a prank. The man threw it to his wife, and as she opened it out tumbled dozens and dozens of bills, totaling well over a thousand dollars.

In the years since then such special blessings have continued unabated. Just this past fall a letter arrived in the mail with a note saying, "We've been wondering how you were making ends meet, but we've decided not to wonder anymore." There was no signature, but there was a bank draft for $4,000.

Then this past Christmas, someone, again anonymously, provided the family with lodging, expense money, and a chauffer-driven car so that they might spend Christmas in Salt Lake City with their daughter, who was again in the hospital.

This was all done anonymously. This family has no idea in the world which of their neighbors and friends have been their benefactors, caring for them all these years.

Imagine, if you will, how this family has been affected. Would they ever dare to be upset with an acquaintance? Would they dare get angry with a neighbor? And you can imagine what their prayers must be like each day as they pray for these anonymous people who are developing the Christlike ability to share without their left hand knowing what their right hand is doing.

7

EVEN ONE SOUL

I beamed with pride and imagined briefly that I might just become another Heber C. Kimball. "What a missionary!" I thought, "What a teacher!" Just three months in the field and already I was watching my first family climb the steps of the chapel on their way to the baptismal font.

It seemed almost too good to be true. Six weeks ago I had approached them with my one somewhat modified "Golden Question." My companion and I had taught them the first lesson that very night and all of them had been home and participated in the discussion. Even Julio, the youngest, had answered our questions intelligently. It seemed as if they had been waiting for us.

Of course, they didn't just accept everything automatically. The Word of Wisdom had been a struggle for them at first and I thought at the time that if it hadn't been for my explanation of the blessings one receives when paying tithing, they would have backed out after that discussion.

Today they would be baptized and tomorrow confirmed members of the Church. The six children ranged in age from ten to nineteen, and the three youngest were all boys and as full of energy and life as only ten-, eleven-, and fourteen-year-old boys can be. Yet in their baptismal interviews each had shown a mature understanding of the gospel plan.

We had stressed to them the significance of baptism and each understood that being baptized could be the beginning of a new life. They all knew that if they truly repented, baptism could be the medium through which their sins would be "washed away." During the interviews my companion and I had knelt with each of the family in turn in private prayer while they asked their Heavenly

Father to forgive them of their past sins and recognize their repentance and desire to begin a new life.

Julio had been especially sincere. "Father in heaven," he had prayed, "I'm sorry that sometimes I fight with my brothers and throw rocks. Please forgive me and let the baptismal waters make me better."

Now as my companion left to make sure the chapel and baptismal font were ready for the services, I accompanied the father and his sons to the dressing room so that we could all dress in the baptismal clothes. I had just finished giving them their white clothes and we were beginning to dress when a shout broke into my thoughts, which at the moment were of home and how proud my parents would be.

"Hey, Pedro, guess what I'm doing today!" It was Julio. He was halfway out the window, standing on tiptoes on one of the benches. He had seen a friend and was anxious to share this occasion with him.

However, I failed to see the need to shout and promptly shouted right back, "Julio, never do that again! Don't you know whose house you're in?"

Julio climbed down from the bench and we all finished dressing in silence. My thoughts returned to my family. My older brother had been an assistant to the mission president.

"I may never be a mission leader," I thought, "but at least I'm baptizing." A minute or two later I was beaming again as I watched "my" family file into the chapel and seat themselves on the front bench. But the smile slowly turned into a frown. There were only seven. Julio was missing.

I hurried out of the chapel and looked angrily up and down the hall. I opened the door to the dressing room and stopped short. There was Julio kneeling on the cold dressing room floor with his head bowed and his arms folded.

"I'm really sorry, Heavenly Father," he said. "I know I promised to be better and already I'm being bad again. Please don't be mad like the elder was because I yelled in your house. I won't ever do it again."

I quickly slipped from the room and waited in the hall. I strangely felt just a few inches shorter and a wave of shame rippled across my face. When Julio came out he was smiling. I put my arm on his shoulder and as we walked up the hallway to the chapel I felt a big knot growing in my throat and I said a silent prayer of my own.

"Please forgive me, Father, for being so vain and so proud,

and—Father, thanks so very much for allowing Julio to be the teacher for a moment, and me the student."

(Edward Platt, "Julio." Used with permission.)

The greatest of all gifts we can give to another person is an understanding of the gospel of Jesus Christ and help and encouragement to accept it and live it fully. Nothing else creates more happiness in a human heart; nothing else has such eternal, lasting value. And as the story you have just read pointed out so aptly, gospel teachers are not always who you expect them to be. The Lord teaches just as easily through the meek and lowly as he does through the educated and highly placed.

In June of 1829, the Lord, through the Prophet Joseph, explained to Oliver Cowdery and David Whitmer the significance of sharing the gospel with others. He said:

> And if it so be that you should labor all your days in crying repentance unto this people, and bring, save it be one soul unto me, how great shall be your joy with him in the kingdom of my Father! (D&C 18:15.)

As you may have noticed, the Lord does not specify *which* people he expects us to bring into fellowship. They may be strangers, friends, or family members. It is almost ironic that while we can boldly introduce the gospel to strangers, most of us find it extremely difficult to approach a close friend. Perhaps this is due to the personal investment we have in a relationship, and we want to go to great lengths not to offend or jeopardize that friendship.

Yet we have found in our lives that when we share the gospel with love, the most positive feelings continually occur! Boldly and humbly caring for our nonmember and inactive member friends enough to share the gospel with them has been the real spiritual highlight of our lives. Not only that, but we have also found these relationships with our friends becoming even deeper and more meaningful as this new dimension is added. One of our students discovered this:

66 "It was our junior year in high school, and Joanie couldn't have been more important in my life. Our friendship was unusual for me, though, because I had never had a best friend who was not a member of the Church. I had always thought that it would be difficult to get close to such a person due to our differences in goals and beliefs. Thank goodness this was not the case with Joanie.

"I will never forget one particular night as we planned to spend the night at my house. We had mentioned religion prior to this time, but never discussed it in depth. For this reason, a conversation of this nature was the furthest thing from my mind as we bounded into bed.

"We were both in a talking mood, and to my surprise, we began intently discussing religion—my religion. She began to ask questions, and so, offering a silent prayer, I ventured to not just answer but plunge headlong into telling her how much a part of my life the gospel is. Then she said something which I will never forget. Turning her head in her freshly fluffed pillow, she said, 'I'm not really sure there is a God.'

"I was stunned! Then, almost without thinking, I blurted, 'Joanie, there is a God! I know there is!' I then shared with her some of my experiences and feelings on prayer and knowing about our Heavenly Father.

"We concluded our discussion a little after four in the morning, and as I drifted off to sleep I knew we were closer than ever before.

"I will never forget the overwhelming excitement I felt as I shared, for the first time, my very own testimony. Some months later Joanie confided to me that she had been praying every day, and had found for herself that God does live! Can you imagine my joy as she tearfully thanked me for caring? In all honesty, this experience made me a new person—a person who will never again be afraid to share my most precious gift." **"**

And now come with us to Vietnam, where Brent had the following experience:

Bruce had been "golden" from the beginning. My companion, Ray Ashby, and I were so excited we could hardly contain ourselves. It was only a matter of weeks before Bruce entered the waters of baptism, and that was only the beginning. The following Sunday we flew with Bruce to Da Nang for our district conference, which was especially exciting because Elder Ezra Taft Benson was presiding over the meetings, so that Bruce was privileged to meet an apostle even in the first week of his membership in the Church.

The meeting began with Elder Benson speaking, after which he opened the meeting to testimony bearing. Immediately Bruce jumped up and headed for the pulpit. For a full fifteen minutes he expounded on being missionaries, and the responsibility which was ours. I was so proud of that guy!

We adjourned for lunch, and at 1:00 P.M. we resumed the meeting so that others could share their testimonies. What happened next was so startling that we could hardly believe our eyes. There was Bruce, once again speaking from the pulpit. He said that the Spirit of the Lord was so strong that he just had to express his testimony to us a second time. Again he admonished us to be diligent in our example as well as our missionary efforts. As he sat down we all knew our charge: to care!

Could we now interject a not-too-often-thought-of thought? One of the most vital purposes of the Church organization is to provide a vehicle for caring. We are given Church callings and priesthood assignments that require us to serve, love, and care about others. When was the last time you saw a man place his hands on his own head and give himself a blessing? Never? Absolutely correct! And the reason is that when a man needs a blessing he calls another priesthood bearer. The Church is to teach us, through our callings, how to serve others. This is not merely a request to serve, but a direct commandment.

As with most commandments, however, obedience brings only joy. Imagine the joy of the four Mutual girls in the first story in this book, as they watched their friend get married.

Even the unattractive are lovely—to those who are willing to love!

" "It was a warm, pleasant afternoon. Hundreds of people dotted the beach. Many were sunbathing in the warm California sun, others were playing games, and the rest of the people were enjoying the water.

"The rest of the people, that is, except for Cindy. Cindy sat all alone. She was rather conspicuous, as she was not wearing the typical beach attire. She was wearing her green polyester pants and top, the outfit I had seen her wear almost every day, everywhere she went. She sat with her head in her hands.

"Perhaps she was wishing she had not come with the other LDS girls on this trip, for she had never really been a part of the group. She was different. All the other girls had families that loved and cared about them. Cindy lived at the Children's Home. Yes, she had a family—but her family didn't care, really didn't care, whether she lived or died.

"She was very much overweight, and in school she qualified

for special education classes. But I knew she was a child of God. Cindy had joined the Church just six months ago, and as president of the Laurel class I had tried to be a friend to her; but had I tried hard enough to help her become accepted?

"I stopped to talk to Cindy. She wouldn't talk. Yet as I sat behind her thinking, tears filled my eyes. I had so many advantages that Cindy never had. For instance, I had a mother who had made sure that I had all the right clothes that I needed for the trip.

"Impulsively I grabbed Cindy's hand, pulling her to her feet. We had passed a Sears store on our way to the beach. It was probably four or five blocks away. I slipped into my jeans as I explained to her that we were going to get her a pair of shorts and a top so that she could enjoy the water.

"I wasn't sure if I had enough money to have much fun on the rest of the trip if I spent it on Cindy, but I would have to make that sacrifice. We hurried to the store. It wasn't easy to find something that would fit her, but finally in the men's department we were able to find a pair of shorts and a t-shirt that fit and looked rather feminine.

"Cindy put the clothes on, and we rushed back to the beach. I felt good, and I could tell that Cindy did, too, as she quickly joined in with the other girls. And that was when I finally learned that being called as Laurel president meant being called to care." **99**

As you read this next account, keep in mind that Church responsibilities are more often fulfilled by simple deeds than by spectacular performances:

66 "While I was in high school I had lots of questions and problems I needed to discuss, and since I wasn't very close to either my mom or my dad, I really didn't have anyone to talk with. Then I was made Laurel president in our ward and I began to work very closely with the Young Women president.

"She was probably about twenty-seven. She had two children to care for and one on the way. She was very active in the Church, in the housing development where she lives, and also in her children's school. Yet she took the time to talk to me despite all the other things she had going in her life.

"She was available night or day. If I got to feeling down or I was really happy or excited about something, I knew that she was always there. I could go to her home at any time and she and her family always made me feel very welcome.

"She was an excellent listener and also a good comforter, advice giver, and cheerer-upper. She was a friend and a teacher, for she showed me what really caring for someone else really is. She is still just like a second mother to me." **"**

One of the most exciting concepts to learn in relation to caring is the change which occurs in the hearts and minds of those being cared for:

" "I'm from an LDS family and ever since I can remember I've gone to church on Sunday.

"My grandmother made most of my sisters' and my clothes. She would really out-do herself with our Sunday dresses. We each had pink chiffon dresses trimmed with yards of lace and ribbon and pink taffeta petticoats to wear underneath. They were our 'princess dresses' and I loved wearing mine and feeling that I looked pretty.

"But as a four-year-old, I only appreciated the prettiness for a few minutes after I put the dress on. As soon as we were in the car on the way to church the lace and taffeta would start scratching my neck and arms. Hot days were the very worst as taffeta does not absorb sweat, which only adds to its scratchiness. Needless to say, I was quite uncomfortable by the time we reached the chapel.

"I could usually endure Junior Sunday School opening exercises, but by the time we separated for classes I was restless, tired of sitting still, and itching all over. I felt that I had suffered enough, so instead of sitting quietly in my class during the lesson, I would usually spend the class hour walking along the back wall, climbing into, out of, and under my stainless steel adult-size folding chair. Or sometimes I would persuade one of the little boys in the class to climb up on the table and jump off with me to see who could jump the farthest. I knew that I shouldn't behave like that and I felt a little guilty, but that didn't stop me and I kept right on doing it.

"A couple of weeks before Christmas my teacher handed out parts for us to memorize for the Christmas program. I ripped my paper up before class was over and persuaded another little boy to do the same. My mother somehow got a copy of it and helped me learn it. I recited it perfectly at the Christmas program.

"The Sunday after the Christmas program my Sunday School teacher met me in the foyer after sacrament meeting and placed in my hands a little present of candy. She said that she had meant to give it to me the week before but hadn't been able to find me after the program so she had saved it to give to me the next week.

"I was surprised that she would save the candy for me, especially after the way I behaved in her class, for I didn't think I deserved it. I knew that I wouldn't have saved candy for any bratty kids if I were the teacher. I was so impressed that she cared about me enough to save candy for me even though I wasn't quiet in class that I quit misbehaving in class and started sitting quietly and listening to the lessons." **"**

No chapter on gospel caring would be complete without an account of the greatest priesthood assignment in the Church—home teaching.

" "As I came home from college in the spring my outlook was bleak. I needed money to return to school in the fall, yet I had no means of earning it. The summer job market just didn't exist that year. I hunted and searched for a job throughout the month of May with no luck. If I couldn't find a job soon I would not be going back to school.

"Then *he* entered the picture. *He* was my home teacher. He cared.

"He was a fireman by profession, but had a small fence construction business on the side. His reputation as a fence builder was unexcelled. His fences were built strong and straight.

"When he discovered my predicament, he set about to correct it. His first step was to hire me. Second, he decided to pay me well; more than I was worth and probably more than he could afford. Then he let me go to work, even though it meant putting his reputation on the line. If I made mistakes which ruined the fences, *he* would be blamed by the customer, not me.

"The first day at work I dropped a roll of barbed wire on my foot. Lost-time accident.

"When he asked me to line up the spots for postholes, the marks I made more resembled a field of gopher holes than a straight fence line.

"After he corrected that mistake, he showed me how to sight the posts into a straight line as I set them. Somehow I did it wrong and after setting fifteen posts, my straight line of posts was going in a different direction than his straight line of postholes.

"But throughout these tribulations, he never lost his temper. Rather, he took me aside to show me my mistakes, and then let me set out to correct them.

"Over the course of the summer I'm sure I caused him many headaches and stretched his nerves to the breaking point. Yet never once did he cause me to feel humiliated or incompetent. I only felt loved.

"That year I earned enough money to return to school. But more important than the money, which has already been spent, was the fact that I learned. I learned a skill which will always be valuable to me. I learned the ways of a kind and loving home teacher. I learned that he cared." **"**

Some of the most difficult people in the Church to warm up to are those whose personal habits are obviously not in accord with gospel standards. A ward mission leader told us this story:

" "During my shift at the steel mill, where I have the responsibility of loading steel products into rail cars and trucks, I noticed that one of the truck drivers, a young man of about thirty-five years, seemed quite troubled. I had known him for some time, but had never known him to act so quiet. In fact, our conversation seemed very strained.

"Concerned, I approached him and asked what was bothering him. His response was startling, to say the least.

" 'Tom, you know I've watched you and have noticed things in your conduct, and I really think you can help me.'

"I was surprised, but I thanked him and assured him that I'd do my best to answer any questions he might have.

" 'Well, Tom, here's my problem. As I've mentioned to you before, I have four young daughters, and they have a wonderful mother. Now my oldest little girl turns eight in two weeks. She wants to be baptized, but she wants me to do it and I just can't.'

"I asked, 'Why not?'

"He answered, 'Oh, you know. I just can't quit smoking and drinking. Also, my language is—well, you know.'

"I thought for a moment before replying. 'Jerry, I know you have these problems, but there is no reason why they can't be solved so that you *can* baptize your little girl.'

"There was another pause in the conversation, and a surprised look spread across Jerry's face.

" 'Tom, do you really think I can do it?' Then he frowned and began to think of other reasons why he wasn't worthy.

"The thing was, each of these reasons were weak, simply excuses. I countered every negative thought with positive proposals such as, 'Jerry, go and talk with your bishop. Tell your little girl you will be proud to baptize her. Tell your sweet wife you are going to do it. Jerry, can you picture in your mind the love and the strength you will gain by baptizing her, by carrying out your promise? Why, to your little girl you are the biggest, the best, the most wonderful man in her whole life. She loves you! And you love her. What better way does she have of expressing that love than by desiring you to baptize her? Jerry, can't you feel that love?'

"Again there was a pause, and then an expression of delight and happiness replaced his forlorn look of misery as he grabbed my hand and shouted, 'Tom, I'll do it!'

"Needless to say, Jerry did all that I suggested, and in due time prepared himself and baptized his daughter. He gained a glimpse of eternity with his family, and I have never seen a happier man." **"**

Caring is a learned personal trait which must be nourished continually or it will die. When President Kimball was a stake president in Arizona, he was confronted with a never-ending line of people with problems. For six months, from one general conference to the next, he struggled to answer those problems, and found himself almost mentally and spiritually exhausted.

"I felt," he recalls today, "like a sponge that had been squeezed until it was dry and vacuum-like. Then, we would come to Salt Lake to conference and, after many sessions here, I would return to Arizona still like the sponge, but one that was heavy with wetness and was dripping.

"I have learned that it is by serving that we learn how to serve." (*Ensign*, December 1974, p. 2.)

We know that loving and caring for other people is not just our duty but also our joy—that love is the purpose of existence. Christ reminded his listeners that the second great commandment is to love our neighbor as ourselves—and then, when asked who our neighbor is, he responded with the story of the Good Samaritan.

The essential elements of that story are:

A Samaritan—a member of an outcast group that was regarded with repugnance by the Jewish majority.

A Jewish man, robbed and beaten and near death—clearly in need.

And this combination turned, not to another incident in the cold war between the two hostile peoples, but rather to a consummate act of kindness: The hated Samaritan took up the man who by custom should be his enemy, carried him to an inn, cared for him, and left money so that the care would continue when he had to move on.

The Savior intended this to be an example of service. And the closer we look at the parable, the more we realize that it was not just an emotional story, but a clear guide for our footsteps, too.

The neighbors were Samaritan and Jew, which tells us that service and love know no boundaries: all humankind are neighbors, when need and opportunity combine.

The Samaritan went out of his way to help, which tells us that service is not limited just to times when it is convenient to serve.

The Samaritan paid in advance for service to continue after he had gone, which tells us that even when we cannot serve in person, we must try to serve as best we can from a distance.

Emotionally, however, the story tells us something else. It tells us that love and service are beautiful; and the tears that come to our eyes when we hear stories of genuine love and unstinted kindness are our souls' echoes of the love of Christ, crying out in recognition of a good act.

Service, however, is not easy. (Certainly the Samaritan paid dearly for the good he did!) Like President Kimball, when we serve others we become weary. We are drained. Our kindness is squeezed out of us drop by drop. And if we do not take care to refill our store of kindness, we may come to find that our giving no longer brings us joy.

Drained by overwork, we may become sensitive to ingratitude, wondering why we bother helping "when no one notices anyway."

Immersed in the service projects we most care about, we may come to feel that other sorts of service are "not as important—*they* need to get their priorities straight!"

Satisfied with a job well done and counting the cost of it in exhausted resources and spent emotions, we may come to feel that we "have done our part—they can't expect us to do any more."

But these attitudes are the result of weariness and temptation. Service doesn't have a quota that must be filled, after which no more is needed. One act of kindness is not "better" than another; only the feeling within the heart of the giver make the acts different in value. And if we serve only for gratitude, then gratitude is our reward: isn't it better to serve as the Lord recommended, being so secret about it that our right hand doesn't suspect what our left hand is doing?

When such feelings come on us, the cure is not to stop serving. Rather, the cure is to refill our sponges; to drink deeply from the fountains the Lord has provided for us, so that our store of kindness never runs dry.

After all, charity knows no limits. It is not a compartment in the life of a good person; children of God have love for their fellow beings as the very backbone of all their behavior. Love is not turned on and off by a switch. It is always on—and our concern is to make sure there's no energy crisis that cuts off our love supply!

8

STORMS

Several years ago I (Blaine) had the opportunity of spending two summers as a counselor at the Treasure Mountain Scout Camp in the Grand Tetons of Wyoming:

Each weekend when the camp was empty, one or two of the counselors were assigned to stay there as a protective measure, hoping in that way to discourage vandalism and other problems.

On one such weekend, when another man and I had drawn the assignment, we spent Sunday morning in our tent reading and talking. Early in the afternoon heavy clouds began rolling up the canyon from the valleys of Idaho, and in a matter of a very few minutes we were in the middle of a real gully-washer. The peaks vanished into the churning clouds and the darkness became so intense that we were forced to light our lantern. The rain came in great sheets that slashed down the slopes above us, tore across our tiny tent, and slammed into the pines beyond.

After an hour the storm passed, and my friend and I ventured outside to view the remains. For some time we walked in silence up among the camps, amazed and a little overwhelmed at what the storm had done. Trees were twisted and torn, branches were scattered around, and Teton Creek had become a raging, muddy torrent.

Out beyond Raven's Roost, one of our farthest camps, we came to a huge dead tree that I had considered cutting down several times but had passed up, not feeling that ambitious. Now, though, the monarch was down, its hundred-foot-plus length stretched across the meadow before us.

I stared in amazement, and at last made some comment about the fury and power of a storm that could wreak so much havoc and bring about such destruction in so short a time. My friend stood silent for a moment before he walked around the great tree to stoop in the grass on its farther side. Quickly I walked over to see what it was that he had found, and was surprised to see him gently shaking the water from the petals of a thick patch of blue forget-me-nots.

"Funny thing," he said, after shaking the water from all of them, "the storm did all this damage around here but didn't hurt these flowers at all. In fact, if anything they look better for the experience."

Storms of adversity are going to occur from time to time whether we wish them to or not, knocking down and blowing over everything they can. The trees that fell did so because they had grown hard and unyielding and so put up too much resistance when the storm came. The flowers, while beaten around a bit by the same storm, were flexible enough while holding their position to come through virtually unscathed.

When the storms of life occur, as they most certainly will, we have but to bow temporarily to their fury while we remain permanently rooted in the gospel, and we will survive. In fact, like the flowers we will do more than survive—we will grow from the experience and gain resources that will help us care for others.

Blaine recalls the experience that most tried our family—yet best prepared us to be strong in the gospel and compassionate to others:

Just shortly after I turned eight years old and was baptized a member of the Church, my father and mother were involved in an auto accident in which my mother lost her life. Dad was thus left a widower with four little children to care for, and we were left motherless and sometimes almost fatherless as Dad buried himself in his work trying to conquer his grief.

My memories of that time are sketchy, for looking back I now see that I turned inward in an attempt to escape my loneliness. As the oldest of the children I felt some responsibility for them, yet I was hurting so badly that my meager attempts to help were usually abortive.

The next few years were dismal ones in my life. Dad married again, the younger sister of my mother, and in the process my two cousins, both older than I, became brother and sister to my own family. I guess I wasn't mature enough then to understand Dad's loneliness, for I grew quite bitter about Mother's death and this new marriage. And the bitterness grew until it seemed like I was always in torment, always miserable, always unhappy, my life always filled with problems.

But then came a night in the spring of my fifteenth year. It began badly enough, for I had one of my customary fights with my new brother, which led to one of my customary arguments with Dad and my new mother, and that ultimately led to my customary banishment to my bedroom.

I retired but somehow couldn't sleep, and for several hours I lay tossing and turning and groaning under the weight of injustice which seemed continually being heaped upon me. I think I was more lonely for my mother that night than I had ever been, and I recall crying out, "Why?" to Heavenly Father over and over again, struggling to understand why he had been so cruel, so unfeeling as to take my mother away from me when I needed her so badly.

At length in desperation I arose and quietly dressed and left the house, not intentionally going anywhere and yet soon realizing that I was traveling a direct course toward the cemetery where Mother was buried. As I walked I started to cry, and I soon found myself running, keeping time with my beating feet and pounding heart to the sobs that I couldn't seem to control.

At the cemetery I threw myself to the ground where I lay numb for what seemed a long time, controlling my sobbing and still asking Heavenly Father over and over again, Why was Mother dead? Why was I so miserable and so lonely? Why? Why? Why?

In time, though, I grew quiet, and as I was lying there I realized that somewhere close by were some irises, flooding the cemetery with their sweet scent. In the moonlight I looked around and quickly discovered that they were growing along the fence just across the road from Mother's grave. I walked over and picked one and took it back to the grave, intending to place it there because I remembered that Mother loved irises so much.

Only for some reason I didn't put it down. Instead, I held it up to my nose, inhaling deeply its sweet aroma. Then I began to examine the flower, each delicate petal filled with dark veins, all fluffy and fuzzy toward the center and yet thinning and spreading as they neared the edge of the petal. It looked so pretty to me in the moonlight.

I guess it was about then that I noticed how quiet it was. For some reason all the night sounds had stopped, and I don't remember ever feeling the quiet so intensely. A mile away a car roared past on the highway, and as its tire-scream faded into the distance the stillness settled even more thoroughly around me.

Clutching the iris closely, I lay back on the grass and noticed the stars for the first time that night. They were somehow different, the Big Dipper not lying comfortably in its normal position. Then I realized that the Big Dipper hadn't changed. It was me. I was seeing them in a different time than I ever had before, and that was why they appeared to have changed.

After a few minutes of star-gazing, I rolled over and began again examining my iris, and I suppose it was at that moment that Heavenly Father chose to bless me with one of the greatest blessings of my life. I remember looking at my flower and thinking that it was perfect, a perfect creation. Then my mind jumped and I felt that I was listening to a perfect silence. Quickly I rolled over and gazed again into eternity, an eternity perfectly organized and perfectly controlled, and suddenly, for the first time since Mother's death, I felt peace, a tremendous sense of contentment and rightness that I knew had come from my Heavenly Father.

Then into my mind jumped a statement that Dad had made many times, that had never until that moment seemed significant. "Heavenly Father is perfect." Now I knew what he meant! God *was* perfect. Everything he did was perfect. My iris was perfect simply because God had designed it to be so. The universe was perfect for the same reason.

And then came the greatest concept of all, one that has influenced my life more than perhaps any other in the years since then: Heavenly Father, being perfect, could not make a mistake. He was incapable of imperfection. Everything he did was right. It had to be!

And suddenly I knew without doubt: Mother's death had not been an accident! Heavenly Father, for reasons that I still do not fully understand, had deemed it wisdom that my mother and Dad's sweetheart be taken into the world of spirits at that point in time. It was not for me to know the reasons, but (and I was crying again as all this wisdom seemed to flood my mind) I *had* been blessed to know that he was perfect, that he loved Dad, my little brother and sisters, myself, and my mother with a perfect love, and it was because of that love that he had allowed her to die.

Heavenly Father did not make mistakes! He wanted us to grow up without her mortal presence, but somehow I knew that we would still feel her love as a spiritual entity, just as real as it had ever been.

There were more thoughts that night. If Heavenly Father loved us and was perfect, then that meant that he loved my step-family also, and wanted them to be a part of us. Who was I to fight a decision that Dad had told me over and over again had been made only because the Lord had told him to make it?

Holding my iris I made my way slowly home in the last darkness before dawn, and it was by far the happiest journey of my life. Somehow, despite my youth, I realized that Heavenly Father had given me a priceless gift that night. Yet years later I am still learning the significance of that gift, the gift of understanding his divine care for me.

We cannot prepare for a crisis after that crisis is upon us. Before we can meet an issue face to face we must have the faith to know and understand that God does indeed love us, and "that all these things shall give thee experience, and shall be for thy good." (D&C 122:7.)

In Proverbs 24:10 we read, "If thou faint in the day of adversity, thy strength is small."

If your own "day of adversity" causes you to stumble and sink into depression, then you may know that your spiritual strength, your faith, is limited. If your outlook remains optimistic and faithful, then your strength is great and you have properly prepared yourself for your day of adversity.

The test of our spirituality does not occur when our spiritual puddle is calm and unruffled. It occurs rather when the winds blow and the waves of suffering arise:

> If thou hast run with the footmen, and they have wearied thee, then how canst thou contend with horses? and if in the land of peace, wherein thou trustedst, they wearied thee, then how wilt thou do in the swelling of Jordan? (Jer. 12:5.)

Christ's suffering cannot be compared to anything we can ever be called upon to suffer, for our agonies are usually private, while his pain was for the sins of everyone in the world. However, two scriptural accounts do teach us of the value of the kind of pain that we who are not divine can suffer in this world.

When Joseph Smith was a prisoner in Liberty Jail, he felt keenly not only his own loneliness and fear, but also the deprivation and suffering of his people. In section 122 of the Doctrine and Covenants, the Lord answers Joseph's prayers by reminding him of all the terrible things that might happen to him—worse, in fact, than those which had already occurred. Then the Lord tells him that all of it would be for his experience, and would do him good; and besides, how could Joseph complain, knowing that Christ himself suffered more than Joseph could imagine, and did it without complaint, but voluntarily, for an exquisitely noble purpose?

And in 2 Corinthians 1:1-11, Paul reveals some of the pain

and sacrifice he had gone through because of his testimony of the Savior. As always, however, Paul sees clearly the reason why God permitted such suffering, and explains to us the great purposes served:

"That we may be able to comfort them which are in any trouble, by the comfort wherewith we ourselves are comforted of God." Who can understand what it is like to sit alongside a friend or loved one dying from some terminal illness? Who knows the heartache of a broken home? Who knows the unrelenting sting of failure? Often we think that no one who has not experienced such things can comprehend them.

But pain is not unique. Even those who have not lost loved ones can know the pain of loneliness. Even those who have a home intact can know the pain of rejection by a loved one. Even those who seem successful have known the shame of having done their best and not achieved; the humiliation of a personal disaster revealed in public.

And even if our own experiences don't prepare us enough to offer comfort, Christ "has descended below them all." Those who are in tune with Christ's love can offer to others the very compassion they have received from Christ. When you have felt the joy of forgiveness for sin because of the suffering of Christ, you gain great wellsprings of comfort that you can in turn offer to those whose particular pain you may not have experienced.

"That we should not trust in ourselves, but in God which raiseth the dead: Who delivered us from so great a death, and doth deliver: in whom we trust that he will yet deliver us." We have suffering in our lives to teach us to trust in God. After all, when our own supposed wisdom or strength is not enough to get us through a difficult time, we have only one place to turn if we are not to despair—to the strength of the Father, the compassion of the Son, the guidance of the Holy Ghost. When we feel we can simply go no farther alone, we don't have to. We can reach out and be led and helped the rest of the way. But if we never have suffering that brings us to a point where we recognize our own insufficiency, how can we learn to rely on the Lord?

"Ye also helping together by prayer for us, that for the gift bestowed upon us by the means of many persons thanks may be given by many on our behalf." So many people try to bottle up their pain and present a bold face to the world—yet it would be so much better if they would shed some of their pride and allow others to help them bear their burden—because, as Paul pointed out, when many are praying (and working and helping) on behalf of a person who is in need, then when their prayers are answered and the suffering is relieved, all have shared together in the pain and all partake of the comfort. When one person's solitary grief is eased, he kneels alone and gives thanks to God. When many people have worked for the sufferer's relief, then all kneel together to give thanks to the Lord, and the suffering has served the vital purpose of drawing many different people together and making them brothers.

But whether suffering does us good or destroys us depends on our reaction. Blaine served in a bishopric in Rexburg, Idaho, in the aftermath of the Teton Dam flood, and from that vantage point he saw all sorts of reaction to that tragedy—a tragedy that, since it cost so few lives and primarily destroyed only property, was relatively minor. He comments as follows:

Some people became very bitter; others were morose and despondent for longer-than-necessary periods of time; yet I know of many who got on their knees and thanked Heavenly Father for the experiences they were gaining.

Interestingly, the numbers who became thankful for the flood grew as the cleanup stretched into weeks and they became aware of the love others had for them, shown as thousands of strangers flocked into town to give of themselves in the cleanup operation. How can one not become thankful when one sees such giving and caring as that?

Can you think back in your mind to the time when you first realized who you were? What kind of a person you were? I can, and it is rather interesting to do it. Very clearly I can see myself as a boy of about five years lying in the moist sand and gravel at the bottom of an irrigation ditch in Sanpete County, Utah, crying bitter, bitter tears. I had lost my first and only silver dollar, and had hunted for it nearly the whole afternoon without results. So there I was in that ditch, without hope and without solace.

I can still feel the gravel, I can see the ants crawling around the small rocks that must have seemed to them boulders, and I can smell the spearmint grass that grew wild along the bank. And all of this is vivid, as though it were only yesterday.

But as I lay there I thought of prayer. I said one of not very great length and crawled out of the ditch and walked right to where my silver dollar lay under the leaves of a cocklebur.

At that point I wondered whether my prayers had been answered; today I know they were. I have had time to think about it since then. I am still fundamentally that boy of five years. Inside of me I feel almost exactly the same as I did then, except that I have added many more experiences to that one. The greatest experiences of our lives, the ones that teach us the greatest lessons, may not be clear to us, even in their most important significance, when they first happen to us. But the Lord has blessed us with a memory so that the experiences are there for us to live with, to keep and treasure and observe and ponder. That way we can evaluate their significance gradually. We don't need to make hasty decisions, such as, "What is happening to me is bad," or "This is happening to me because I have sinned." Such conclusions, made in haste, may be erroneous.

As we walk through life we do so with all our years trailing along behind us. In a moment of leisure, in a moment of meditation, we are back in a certain experience, learning from an old trial the lesson that will help us endure a new one.

And the longer we live, the longer grows our train of experiences. (And, by the way, isn't this an interesting motivation for keeping a journal? Perhaps the most important reason of all is just to aid our memories of our lessons in life so we can continually grow from them.)

There are many many examples of trials that could be included here, and we will relate a few, but it should be pointed out that no two people will have exactly the same kinds of storms in their lives. We are all different and so will be affected by different kinds of adversity. And it is good to expect that.

In thinking of trials, we always recall the severe tests the pioneers had, in being driven from their homes, persecuted for their religion, forced to cross fifteen hundred miles of wilderness, required to set up homes in an even greater wilderness, and so on. But they endured another kind of trial also, one that we seldom hear of, and one that is much more modern than we tend to think.

In *Great Basin Kingdom*, written by Leonard Arrington, we read of President Brigham Young's strong suggestion in the 1850s that the members of the Church dispense with anything they could not make for themselves. Along with these instructions he set in motion the machinery of Churchwide manufacturing, so that vital items would not have to be purchased outside. Under this program were established such things as a pottery factory, a paper mill, a sugar mill, a woolen mill, an iron mine and foundry, a lead mine, and a cotton industry. With the exception of the paper mill, all these enterprises failed, at least for a while, and did so at great losses to the Saints, both individually and collectively.

For instance, the pottery factory produced no pottery and cost about $12,000—a lot of money in 1853. The sugar industry cost many members ten years of work, acres and acres of beets planted that could not be sold, and about $100,000 in capital loss.

The iron mine and foundry also cost ten years of hard labor by many members, and its capital loss was over $150,000. The lead mine also failed to be profitable, and it is interesting to note that it failed right on the spot where the fabulous Potosi silver mine was discovered by non-Mormons not ten years later; while the iron mission failed on a mountain of 200,000,000 tons of 52 percent iron ore.

It is obvious that the Lord was not so concerned with the financial success of these ventures as he was with their social and spiritual success. The lesson he seems from our 20th-century perspective to have wanted the Saints to learn was one of brotherhood, of unity, of cooperation, of caring for each other, and that lesson could apparently be taught more effectively through economic hardship than through success. In this day, when so much stress is placed on economic achievement, aren't there some interesting lessons we can learn from the experiences of our forebears? Is it truly important that we all be financially successful?

Many years ago, I failed in a business venture. My cash was gone and I was behind in my rent. My family was not getting proper food. My first thought, of course, was to get a job, but this turned out to be more difficult than I had anticipated. Other businesses were also folding.

Things went from bad to worse. I ran the gamut from feeling sorry for myself to trying to reaffirm my faith in myself. I tried to mix with successful people and attended inspirational lectures to try to keep my confidence up.

I called on one business firm after another in an effort to obtain a job. When I was refused, I left with bitterness. Then I got to the point of not actually expecting to be hired. This attitude got the natural results. I became short-tempered with my family; in short—I became a regular heel.

Then one day as I was driving home after one more defeat with a prospective employer, I stopped at a crosswalk to let a youngster pass. I raced my engine in anger for he was intolerably slow. Then I looked at him. This was no ordinary boy. He wore a grey and blue baseball suit. He carried a bat on his shoulder and onto the bat was laced a glove. I could see the outline of a baseball in his pocket. He wore his baseball cap at a jaunty angle. He was every inch a big-league baseball player.

Tears welled in my eyes as he slowly crossed the street. The boy was terribly clubfooted and could hardly drag his body across the walk. He smiled and waved me on, but I did not smile back at him. I just sat there, feeling terribly ashamed, until a horn in back of me bade me go forward. This little fellow, struggling across the street, had envisioned himself as a great baseball player. He had the greatest of hope. He *was* a baseball player. I silently said a prayer for the boy and drove on.

The next day, I found a job and began enjoying myself in the work I know best. The sight of that happy crippled boy had, when I was finally ready, transformed me into a man. (Albert R. Johnson, *Success Unlimited,* June 1970.)

We are going to have many kinds of storms buffet our lives, and we will have them off and on as long as we are here as mortals. Perhaps, instead of involving money, they will cost us physical pain, as in the following account, where caring was learned and can now be shared.

Blaine's wife Kathy relates the following experience:

" "As we were awaiting the birth of our sixth child, we grew very impatient as it seemed to take forever. I had been delivery size for several months, having carried huge amounts of water, so I was quite miserable and anxious for the arrival of this new baby. Of course we were counting on a girl after one girl and then four boys in a row. Our one daughter was counting on a little sister also.

"The day finally came, only complications developed as labor advanced. My husband and our bishop administered to me then, and things seemed well until my uterus ruptured during the more advanced stages of labor. The problem was that I was hemorrhaging internally and so no one could tell for certain what was wrong. The only sign at first was that the baby's heartbeat was getting slower and slower. They finally rushed us into the delivery room in order to speed things up and get the baby out. Her heartbeat completely stopped before she was born, but they were able to work with her and get her breathing again. We felt that that was an indescribable blessing to us.

Not knowing anything was wrong with me, the doctor sent me back to my room, where a short time later I passed out. My blood pressure then dropped extremely low, and not knowing what was wrong but knowing at least that I needed blood, they started intravenous treatment.

"In a short time I regained consciousness only to find myself in almost unbearable pain, a pain that was so intense that the slightest touch on my body sent me into muscle spasms. This pain lasted through the rest of the day and all through the night.

104

"It was during this time that I became aware just how many people really cared for me, and it was this showing of love and concern that gave me the strength to endure all that I did. My doctor was very concerned, and stayed with me much of the time, trying to help me. The nurses, one after another, stayed by my side giving me comfort and doing as much for me as they could. My wonderful husband, who I know worried and suffered terribly during this time, stayed by my bedside all during that night, reassuring me that everything would be all right because when they gave me the blessing I was blessed that both the baby and I would be healthy and strong.

"Only once did I actually think that I might not make it, and that was after my doctor called in a specialist the next morning at 6:00. He determined very quickly what was wrong and what would have to happen. Surgery and that would mean, of course, no more children in our family. The hospital personnel could not figure out how I survived my ordeal, except to say that someone else, not visible to them, had been with me and with them. My wonderful friends and relatives sent cards and flowers and words to help and comfort me, and I am so thankful for them. My love for them simply cannot be put into words.

"My mother and father too were a great help. While all this was taking place my mother was coming to us on a bus so she could be there to help. She stayed with my family taking care of them, fixing meals, washing, ironing, and doing everything that goes with a big family of small people, for two weeks, which was a great comfort to me.

"After my mother left my niece came to live with us and to help us out, since I was unable to do much. She was just a teenager, but not thinking of herself in the least she dropped everything to help us. Not one time did I ever hear anything from her but encouragement and thankfulness that she could be there.

"The greatest gift I received, however, was a much deeper love and appreciation for our Savior during that night, that long lonely night. I prayed continually for help, and somehow realized that this was nothing compared to what he had gone through for me. Oh, how I wish I could let everyone feel and understand what I felt and understood that night, and have them know how much he cares for them! He cared enough for me to let me suffer and feel those things so that I might appreciate my life more, and appreciate my husband, family, and friends—and especially him.

"I have thought over and over about what I can do to show my love and appreciation for our Savior and all the wonderful people who helped me. I have concluded that all I can do is to labor continually the rest of my life in the service of others, building them up and helping them in any way that I can, and this I will do as long as I can." **"**

Pain often teaches people about caring, particularly when people showed caring to the sufferer. Another type of storm that may buffet us does not involve personal pain so much as the anguish of watching a loved one suffer. And who is to say which is the most difficult kind of pain to bear?

As Mormons we don't like to talk about divorce very much, because with our heavy emphasis on successful family life we see divorce as a failure. And so it is, and under most conditions we do not support it. But that doesn't seem to stop it from occurring within the Church, and much more frequently than we would like.

How do we view these people whose marriages have failed? Within the structure of the Church, how do we treat them? Many of them, of course, have bungled their marriages because of their own foolishness or waywardness, but there are just as many who were honestly trying to do their best and have become victims of eternally foolish partners. Yet they all suffer alike, and almost universally (within the Church) they view themselves as failures who are not quite so good as others.

Do our acts and statements and thoughtless conversations contribute to their feelings of inferiority and failure? Or are we Christian enough to care these people into positive self-images and to let them know that we love them just as much now as we did before?

" "My little sister was getting a divorce! It was hard to believe. Things like this happened in other families, but not in ours. I kept asking myself what had gone wrong. From the outside everything looked rosy. She always had a smile on her face, a nice comfortable home, two lovely children, nice clothes, and plenty of money. They often took weekend trips together. It seemed to me that she had everything, and so I found it difficult to believe that she would leave her husband.

"She said very little to us about the reasons for the divorce. She just wanted us to understand and know that she had very valid reasons for leaving, though she was so independent that she wouldn't talk about them with any of us.

"The divorce went through easily, and the real reasons for it came out in the hearing. These reasons made my mother understand what her daughter had been through the last several years, and she then felt that her daughter had acted wisely in getting a divorce. My mother even said that my sister should have left her husband a long time ago.

"My sister's difficulties really brought the rest of our family together. We all wanted to help her, but what could we do? She didn't want our help. She wanted to do it on her own. She wanted to prove to herself that she wasn't a failure. It even seemed like she avoided us.

"We prayed for her a lot, but it seemed like our prayers were going unheard, and we couldn't understand why the Lord wasn't listening. It seemed that all we could do was to offer help, keep praying, and tell her as often as we could that we still cared.

"After a while she did move closer to home. She easily found an apartment, job, and babysitter, and she seemed to perk up a bit. None of us will ever really understand what she went through: the sleepless nights, the fears of whether she'd get through the next day with her sanity. It was especially hard for her to leave her little children each day, but she had to if they were going to eat. I used to go have lunch with her, and sometimes she would let down her barriers and I would realize things weren't going well, though she really tried to pretend they were.

"It got harder and harder for her to make ends meet. My folks tried to help with car repair bills, food, and extra money, but it just wasn't working out. Whenever our family got together she was all we talked about. We held family councils and family prayers, we prayed in our own families, and all of us fasted quite a bit in her behalf.

"And then she met a girl at work who really seemed to understand her problems. This woman had some problems of her own, and it seemed that they really hit it off well, talking out and trying to understand each other's problems.

"Then this woman introduced my sister to a man she knew who had also been divorced, and they seemed to be good for each other. She became like a new person, with a little sparkle in her eyes, something that had been missing for a long time.

"Not long ago she and this man were married, and she says it is so good to feel like a real person again. Her husband is good to her and to her two little children.

"I know that the Lord did answer our prayers. It took time to work out all the problems involved, and they have not all been taken care of as well as we would like, but at least the four of them seem happy.

"Our whole family has learned a lot from this experience. Did we really love each other as much as we had thought we did? I know that we have all grown closer and learned how important it is to trust each other and stick together and love each other no matter what.

"We have also learned how important it is to let other people help you when you need help. That is all part of caring, and that way everybody can grow and learn to be their brother's keeper. And now we are still praying that my sister and her little family will want to become part of the Church again." **"**

In this story there are hints of several kinds of storms, but the one that must cause as much personal and private anguish throughout the Church as any other is the trial of having a loved one choose to reject the principles of the gospel. This may result in inactivity of various degrees and lengths of time, or it may lead to disfellowshipment or excommunication, depending upon the nature of the transgression and the desires of the individual involved. This is not an easy storm to weather, and it is equally difficult for the individual involved and for his or her loved ones:

" "I have always been active in the Church. All my life I have attended all my meetings, paid a full tithing and every other donation asked of me, and served willingly in the positions I have been called to. I don't mean to sound like I think I'm perfect, for better than anyone else I know that I am not. But I have always had a testimony of the gospel and have done my best to live it as it should be lived.

"Ever since I was a little girl I have longed for a temple marriage and a celestial family. I have planned out in my mind the kind of a man I wanted to marry. These have been my dreams and my goals. And they all came to pass, just as I had prayed for them to do. My husband was a wonderful man, a returned missionary, and he held many positions of leadership and service in the Church, including being part of a bishopric. We had several children, and I felt that we had a very special life together.

"Then it happened. He was excommunicated from the Church, and since then all of us have lived in a terrible kind of misery that I can't describe and doubt anyone else who has not experienced it can understand.

"At this point my husband does not seem at all repentant, and

I am torn in my feelings between wanting to throw him out because of his miserable spirit and negative effect on the children, and holding onto him because of the love we once had and that I still have, and the almost certain feeling that if I do ask him to leave then that will be it as far as his salvation is concerned. In other words, perhaps his family is the only hope he has left. I have prayed and prayed about this, and finally feel that the decision, when and if it is made, should not be made by me.

"The biggest problem I have had, or one of them at least, has been learning to like myself again. In the Church there is so much stress placed on successful marriages and so much feeling that if you fail it is the fault of both parties that it is difficult to feel or think otherwise. So I have been eaten with so much guilt that it has almost destroyed me. Yet the Spirit has whispered to me that the fault is not mine, that he chose willingly to sin and must now suffer for that transgression, and that I must continue to live my life and teach my children within the framework of the gospel. I have freely forgiven him and have continued to love him throughout the whole ordeal, though as he falls farther away from what I hold dear it is becoming increasingly difficult.

"I have survived and am still here because of two things, the absolute comfort of prayer and the love and caring of my ward members. I am new in my ward, and many of the people don't even really know me, yet I am constantly aware of their love and acceptance, and lean on them spiritually and emotionally.

"Through this my testimony of the Savior has grown, and so has my testimony of the adversary, who seems to try harder to tear apart strong homes than weak ones. Even Saints with happy homes should never get too confident and hide their heads and think they are out of reach. They are not!

"I have thought, 'Why can't I make him repent through my faith and prayers?' But I have been told that that isn't the way. If he is to repent it must be because he wants to do so. It must come from within him.

"So now I lean on the members of the Church, and most importantly I lean upon the Lord, for I know he will not let me down. He is my rock, and I know that someday I will be able to understand why we have experienced all this suffering." **"**

In a hospital a doctor removes a man's leg or arm because of serious damage to the tissue or bone. Does the doctor then place him on a bed, shove him out the door and into the street, and shout: "Good luck! Remember, we love you, and pray that you will make it back OK!" Of course he doesn't. The amputee is given every bit of care available to insure that he will heal and return as quickly as possible to normal society.

Are not the spiritual amputees in our Church worthy of as much care? Definitely they have sinned, and definitely they must repent. But wouldn't that repentance be much more likely or more certain if they knew that we as members still loved them and still cared for them?

There seems to be a tendency for many of us to feel that a person who has been excommunicated has somehow just been removed from the human race, to feel for some reason that his needs have changed and he is an alien creature that must be shunned. How sad that such an attitude exists! When a man is excommunicated, does he suddenly lose his need to feel loved, or to associate with good people? Not at all! Especially not then! Yet there is a feeling in some circles that if the man's employer is a Mormon he must also be fired, as if his family no longer needed to eat.

Excommunication is not a sin! The sin occurred previously, and excommunication is one of the steps that will lead to repentance. Both of the authors have been part of several Church courts, yet neither of us has ever sat in a court where any feelings other than absolute love and concern for the salvation of the transgressor have been manifested. And, incidentally, neither of us has ever sat in a court where the decision as to the action to be taken was a decision of the priesthood leaders present. That decision has always been directed by the Spirit.

The Lord knows his children, good and bad, and knows what things will best promote the chances of their salvation. Thus Heavenly Father, because of his perfect love, has established in his Church devices of love that will enable transgressors to become cleansed of their sins and made pure and spotless so that they might return to his presence. And repentance is possible to almost every person, even if his sin is so grave as to cut him off, for a time, from the Church.

So what is our obligation to these spiritual amputees? An arm around a shoulder can feel like a transfusion of genuine love and can help save an individual who might otherwise have bled to death spiritually after such surgery.

In the Doctrine and Covenants we are told that it is our duty to forgive all men. (D&C 64:10.) That is especially so when the excommunicant has not personally caused us harm. No matter how bad a person acts, no matter how far off the track he may wander, it is our duty and obligation to love him continually. It just may be that our bit of caring is the tourniquet that saves his spiritual life.

" "My brother was the first of our family to join the Church, and for years he labored with the rest of us, trying to get us to join. He was finally successful and baptized myself and my parents. He was married in the temple, but for some reason he withdrew from his family and expressed less affection for them as the years passed. Then his job changed and they moved to a new area, and an innocent affection for a woman at his new job quickly became no longer innocent.

"He was excommunicated from the Church, divorced his wife, and married this other woman. Our family was heartsick, and all of us worked with him and labored in prayer that he might see the error of his ways and regain what he had lost.

"It took nearly five years of constant struggle for him, but he finally realized that the woman he had married was not as she had represented herself to be. He was then able to recognize his mistake and his folly, and humble himself to the point where he could repent.

"He and his new wife divorced and he returned, fully repentant, to his old family. Working carefully with his priesthood leaders and the General Authorities to totally change, he was finally allowed to be rebaptized into the Church, and eventually he had all his blessings restored to him. Our family is convinced that we have witnessed the ultimate in Heavenly Father's love and compassion, and we will all be eternally thankful for the merciful atonement of Jesus Christ." **"**

Many times we bring on our own storms through neglect of some eternal principle, and a kind and wise Heavenly Father allows us to go through the storm that we might learn and thus draw closer to him.

" "Several years ago I was home with two youngsters who were sick all the time (at least it seemed like it), while my husband was absent for up to eighty hours a week in a stressful, high-pressure job. Something very vital was missing in my life, and I had no idea what. But I yearned for a stability and purpose that was lacking. My husband barely had the emotional strength or time to sustain himself, let alone my great needs. I became ill, losing three to four pounds a month.

"Then someone was sent to me from a loving and caring Father: a neighbor, older than I, and very unselfish, intuitive, and wise. She and her husband were busy in Church work and she had six children of her own. She also worked part-time as a nurse. Her life was full and busy, but never too busy to help someone in need, including me.

"I bared my very soul—those deep inner feelings that few of us are able to share with another earthly person—those feelings that are not always beautiful and pleasant. She took my troubled heart and one by one we faced my problems. She worked with me on a daily basis. With the many pressures in her own life it must have been an enormous strain on her, this time-consuming emotional involvement with another to whom she owed no special time nor had any link with other than both being children of a Heavenly Father and Mother. But this was enough for her. She saw a person in need and she gave more than she had.

"After approximately two years of this almost daily caring, my identity was very well defined. I came to know and really understand that I was a daughter of a Heavenly Father who had sent me here on a mission, who gave me prior knowledge of my personal trials and the problems I would encounter upon the earth. My connecting link was Jesus Christ. He is always there! He is always listening! He is always loving! He is always helping!

"My friend gently cut loose my dependence on her and showed me through her example a Christ-centered life. Great new meaning came into my life. I spent some twenty years searching, and now that I have come to know the Savior, I am beginning to reach out and share this great gift. My friend loved and cared and shared, and now I am trying to do the same." **99**

Each of these accounts comes down finally to one point of focus: To survive, all of those who suffered turned finally to Jesus Christ.

In Alma 39, the prophet talks to his son Corianton, who had neglected his missionary work and left his field of labor to chase after the harlot Isabel. As a grief-stricken father who knew better than most others the pain of sin, Alma taught his young son the terrible seriousness of his immorality and exhorted him over and over again to repent. Then in verses 12 through 19 Alma concludes his testimony with a rather remarkable lesson. He bears testimony that Christ shall come to take away the sins of the world, points out that that was the message Corianton had been sent to declare, and then perceives through the Spirit that his son is still unsure in his heart about the veracity of Christ's eventual birth and atonement. *Corianton did not have a testimony of Jesus Christ and his mission, and this was why he fell.*

It is that simple, and our problems even today are that easy and yet maddeningly difficult to solve. As the people you have read about have done, we also need to place Jesus Christ in the center of our lives. Then and only then will we be able to safely weather the storms that will come in our lives and help others to do the same.

Now what exactly do we mean by placing Christ in the center of your life? It is this simple. Make him and his mission the thing of most importance to you in everything you do, all day long, every day. Sometimes we find ourselves placing other things in the center, such as family, work, friends, hobbies, fun, recreation, a car, sports, or a Church calling. None of them will work. With anything other than Christ in the center our life will be out of balance, and then when the storm comes and the wind blows it will be inevitable that we eventually topple and fall.

Let us end this chapter as we began it, with an experience of Blaine's: Last night my wife and I left work on this chapter to attend the temple with some of the people in our ward. On our way there we pulled up to a stop sign and were about ready to pull out when a man in a truck smashed into the rear of our car, throwing us forward and giving us quite a jolt.

As I jumped out and ran back to determine the damage, he fell out and staggered forward—very, very drunk. I quickly determined that he had done a great deal of damage to our car. But there were many cars waiting in line and anxious to move, so I suggested that we pull off the road and discuss things. He agreed, I pulled over, and he sped around me and took off up a one-way street the wrong way, narrowly missing another car and quickly disappearing. I tried to catch him and couldn't. Neither did I know his name or get his license plate number.

So there I sat, ready for the temple physically but very angry and frustrated inside, for there was nothing that I could do to find the culprit, nothing at all.

Well, we did go to the temple, the peaceful spirit there began to soothe mine, and as the session progressed I became gradually aware that Heavenly Father was caring, trying to teach me a lesson, just a little lesson that needs to be mentioned in closing here. In the storms that we suffer, such as that little tempest last night, we will not always see justice done. Many times unfairness will prevail, and may continue to do so for years, perhaps our entire life. And if it does we must have the faith to not become bitter, but to believe that all will ultimately be as it should be.

When Alma and Amulek were on their mission to Ammonihah, the wicked people imprisoned them and forced them to watch as the wives and children of the men who were believers were cast into a great fire, where they were destroyed. Amulek cried out against the injustice of the deed, but Alma refused to use his priesthood power to save them. He explained to Amulek:

> . . . The Spirit constraineth me that I must not stretch forth mine hand; for behold the Lord receiveth them up unto himself, in glory; and he doth suffer that they may do this thing, or that the people may do this thing unto them, according to the hardness of their hearts, that the judgments which he shall exercise upon them in his wrath may be just; and the blood of the innocent shall stand as a witness against them, yea, and cry mightily against them at the last day. (Al. 14:11.)

This takes great faith to understand, but it is nevertheless as real as can be. Justice will always prevail, but it may not be up to us to see that it does so immediately. So when a storm comes to your life, instead of weeping over the injustice of it, it is far better to use the experience as a steppingstone to becoming a stronger, more compassionate, more Christlike person.

"And we know that all things work together for good to them that love God, to them who are the called according to his purpose." (Rom. 8:28.)

9

THE GREATEST GIFT OF ALL

Despite our amazing technological achievements, we have only found two ways that are available to all of us of seeing back into history.

The first of these methods requires nothing more than fair vision and a clear night. Once you have that, simply step outside and glance upward at the stars. When you do, you will be gazing backward in time millions and millions of years. You see, the light your eyes behold as starlight actually left those stars that long ago, and it has taken that many years for the light to get here. In reality, those stars we see may not even be there any longer, but the light that would tell us of that has not arrived yet, and may not for another million years or so.

Thinking of that does make the lifespan of a man seem a bit insignificant, does it not? It should also give us a little better idea concerning the magnitude of God's creative ability.

The second way of traveling through time is a great deal more vivid, for we can see whatever we wish to see—when we do our traveling in our minds, we can go as far as we choose and as rapidly as we wish to go. All we need is a bit of knowledge and a good imagination and we're on our way.

So you can come with us as we go back in our minds about nineteen hundred and forty-five years or so. Are you with us? Good, let's get moving.

Oops, watch out for that little brook. We've changed time zones, and in the dark some of us almost stepped into the water. We are going to climb that hill before us, but don't worry, it isn't too steep. That's good. Now right here is a gate, and beyond the gate a garden. This garden, instead of fruits and vegetables, grows mostly rocks and dirt and here and there an olive tree.

Now let's move forward quietly. There are three men sleeping on the ground. They look tired—be careful not to wake them.

In the darkness before us we hear talking—no, pleading. Someone is undergoing some sort of dreadful experience, and he sounds distraught, terribly burdened with some excruciating weight. If we get a bit closer perhaps we can help.

There he is, lying there on the ground in the dust, groaning in an agony of spirit such as we have never seen. We want to move forward, to help him to his feet, but somehow we realize that the pain he is suffering he must suffer alone.

His robes must have been at one time white, but we see now that they are saturated with blood, blood that has been pushed from every pore of his body by the intensity of his physical suffering, and blood that has now mingled with the dust of the earth to give him an appearance such as we have never seen depicted in paintings.

But now the agony is over for a time. Jesus rises to his feet and walks past us to awaken his three companions. In the distance we see leaving Jerusalem a huge throng of people bearing torches, and in the stillness of the night we can hear their shouts and oaths as they approach.

A man walks forward and kisses the Savior. Suddenly one of the men who had been asleep draws his sword and cuts off an ear of one of the torchbearers. Jesus calmly restores it and rebukes his follower for fighting with his sword. Jesus is then taken and led away.

It is now just after midnight; the day is Friday, and we are standing in the vestibule of the home of Annas, the father-in-law of Caiaphas, the Jewish High Priest. Our Savior is also standing there before us, now bound with ropes, and we watch as one of Annas's hired men reaches out and viciously strikes Jesus on the mouth.

He is led away, and we follow to the home of Caiaphas, where we sit for five long hours as priest after priest of the Sanhedrin questions and mocks him, and seeks false witness against him. He is smitten over and over, spat upon, and demanded to give signs of his divinity, and we begin to wonder how any man can stand so much.

At last Caiaphas asks him directly if he is the Son of God. Jesus answers, "Yes," and bears testimony of his future glory. Caiaphas then tears his own clothes, and, astounded, we hear the Sanhedrin pass judgment. Jesus is condemned to *death*.

At daylight another trial proceeds, though this one is mere mockery, a copy of the one held all through the night. The judgment is the same. Through most of the questioning Jesus stands silent, above their satanic taunting. At the end, though, he again bears testimony of his divinity and we wonder how anyone can doubt him.

Then, just as we are about to leave and move to Pilate's residence, someone brings word that one of Jesus' disciples has killed himself, and even now is lying dead in the potter's field. We look at Jesus and are surprised to see tears of pity in his eyes.

In Pilate's court the Roman governor questions Jesus. Interestingly, Jesus answers him, though he will no longer speak to the Jews. Pilate, however, seems perplexed, and upon learning that Herod is in town sends Jesus there, not wishing to assume any responsibility for this man that seems to him so innocent.

At Herod's we find the king happy and excited that he has now seen Jesus, and he is doing his best to get Jesus to perform some miracle. Yet Jesus remains mute, and Herod can only look at the face of the Savior; he is not permitted to hear the Savior's voice. Angered, Herod allows his soldiers to mock Christ and place a royal robe on his back. Still he stands silent, and Herod sends him back to Pilate; we follow.

Pilate, now convinced of Jesus' innocence, does his best to release him without causing too many political problems. Having in custody Barabbas, a murderer, he offers the crowd either his or Jesus' freedom. The crowd, undoubtedly packed with zealot supporters of the Sanhedrin, chooses Barabbas.

In his next effort to appease the people without killing Christ, Pilate decides to physically chastise him in front of the mob. Accordingly Jesus is stripped, bound to a pillar, and scourged. Then the soldiers place on his back a scarlet robe and on his head a crown of thorns, which they drive in place by striking repeatedly with a reed. This reed they then place in his hand, and in mockery they bow down, then stand and file past him, smiting him and spitting on him as they do so.

Now Pilate leads him to the people, hoping that they will take pity. But no, they shout to have him crucified. Pilate, seeing that he cannot convince them otherwise, agrees to their demands. Just at this point we see Claudia, wife of Pilate, come in and whisper in her husband's ear, and the rumor flies that she has had a dream in which she has learned that Jesus is indeed the Son of God.

Pilate, inwardly afraid, pleads again with Jesus to tell who he is. Jesus ignores him, so Pilate reminds him that he, Pilate, has power to have him killed. Jesus now tells him that any power he has over him is given from above.

Now very afraid, Pilate pleads again with the people, who refuse to change their demands. He has washed his hands of the affair, and now he gives in to the people, who cry out, "Let his blood come upon us and our children."

We follow now in the crowd as Christ is led out of the city, bearing the beam for his cross, and stumbles his way toward Golgotha, Place of the Skull. He is very weak, though, and again and again he falls. A soldier, losing patience, grabs a bystander and forces him to carry the cross. He then drags Jesus to his feet and shoves him ahead, forcing him to hurry.

At the hill the Savior is stripped naked and thrown down upon the cross-beam, where a soldier places his foot upon his arm and quickly drives an iron spike through the base of his hand. Without mercy the soldier stretches out his other arm and drives a spike through that hand also, severing the great median nerve that controls the movements of his hands. And we, recalling the last time a dentist touched a nerve in our tooth, can't help but realize that all our pain was caused by a nerve so small as to be unseen, while the nerves severed in Christ's wrists are nearly as thick as a pencil. It is no wonder that he is already in great pain.

Then several men take hold of the beam and raise it roughly into place on the upright of the cross, and after it is secured a soldier takes hold of the dangling feet and nails them together into the wood, one on top of the other. They now stand back to watch and to mock, as do many in the crowd, who come forward and taunt him and spit upon him, mocking his nakedness and his helplessness.

The crucifixion is more terrible than anything we have ever imagined, and sick at heart and in spirit we return to the present. But the present has changed, for in our minds is the vivid sight of Jesus Christ suffering for us, first in Gethsemane, next in Jerusalem, and finally on Golgotha.

On this one journey we have seen greater suffering than has ever been endured by any other human being, either before or since. And the question comes to our minds: Why would any man be willing to give so much for so long with so little personal reward?

And then the answer comes, almost as quickly, for we have been taught it since we were very tiny and have learned it well: Because he loves us.

Because he loves us!

And then we smile and relax, for now we think we totally understand. He loves us and so gave his life as a ransom that he might bring us eventually back into the presence of God, providing resurrection for all mankind and salvation for those who believe in him and keep his commandments.

Very good. But is it enough? Do we who have been taught the gospel all our lives really understand? and implement? What price, really, the atonement? What gifts, actually, were given to mankind during that weekend in Jerusalem, and during the nearly thirty-four years previously?

In seminary one day the question was asked, half mockingly, "Can you draw each one of us?" There was only a moment's hesitation, and then a portrait of each and every student there was sketched, and remarkable as it may seem, that portrait fits every other member of the Church the authors know. Your portrait is at Figure 1.

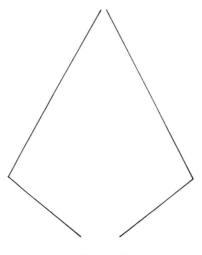

Figure 1

Do you recognize yourself? If not, you should realize that it is a time portrait rather than a photographic or instantaneous one. It starts at birth, then goes outward to age eight, or at whatever age you entered the waters of baptism, and then moves forward in time to perhaps the present moment in your life.

Now we will draw the portrait again, and this time we will add a bit of explanation.

At the waters of baptism we take upon ourself the name of Christ, and agree to keep all his commandments. But at age eight our understanding is pretty limited, also our knowledge. Thus there are many things we do that are contrary to the commandments. And we do them without suffering severe punishment simply because of our lack of understanding. (Figure 2.)

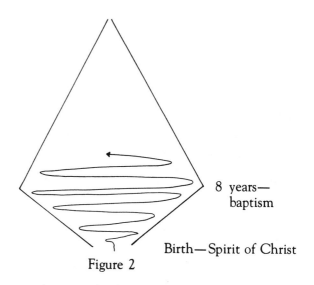

8 years—
baptism

Birth—Spirit of Christ

Figure 2

As we move up the triangle, however, we are progressing in both time and understanding, and so our freedom to make mistakes without serious consequence becomes progressively more limited. As an example, an eight-year-old boy is tempted beyond endurance by an article in a store that doesn't belong to him. He takes it and is caught. What most likely will be his punishment? Perhaps some fairly strong chastisement from home and a lecture by an authoritative figure such as a policeman.

Now suppose a sixteen-year-old has the same experience and is also caught. At sixteen it will no longer be a spanking and a lecture; it will be a criminal charge and a juvenile court record.

As another example, if a young person within the Church transgresses the laws of morality, he must go through a very strict program of repentance, but only in the case of flagrant violation and defiant attitude will a Church court be held. On the other hand, if a man or a woman who has been through the temple commits the same sin a court must always be held, and the process of repentance is much more painful and time-consuming.

You see, the older we get and the more experience we have, the more control we are expected to exercise over ourselves. So as an adult, your portrait now looks like this.

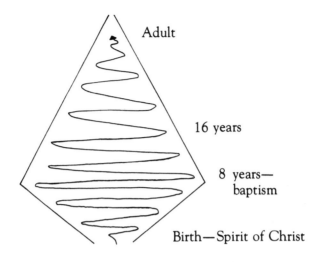

Adult

16 years

8 years—
baptism

Birth—Spirit of Christ

Figure 3

And now we come to the "Mormon Syndrome." To explain the origin of this strange malady, let us go back to the time when we were very small, to when we first began to learn of the commandments given us by Heavenly Father, Remember them? Don't steal, don't tell lies, don't be mean. As we got a little older others were added, such as not using profanity, keeping the Word of Wisdom, remaining morally clean, paying a full tithing. Even later we learned of budgets and building funds, honesty in our business dealings, faithfulness in Church callings, obedience to covenants, kindness to husbands, wives, and children, and all the other laws, ordinances, contracts, statutes, judgments, decrees, revelations, and requirements which come to man from God.

All these seem to come upon us suddenly, as does adulthood with its attendant responsibilities, and it is a very rare person who is well prepared for them all. And only Jesus Christ mastered them, in total, in his first effort to do so.

A syndrome is a series or group of signs or symptoms that indicate a particular problem. The particular problem of the "Mormon Syndrome" is how we mentally and emotionally view the commandments of God. If we view them as objects of impediment, stumbling blocks in the path leading to what *we* want to do, principles to fight against or get around, as most of us do at one time or another, then we suffer the "Mormon Syndrome."

The Word of Wisdom (D&C 89) was given by the Lord in February 1833. None of us has been around as long as it has, implying that all of us (unless we are converts from outside the Church) have heard about it since we were very small. Yet how many people do you know who still perceive the Word of Wisdom as a stumbling block to their fun, an impediment to their happiness? This would include the old man in the Church who sneaks down to the corner tavern in the evening for a little nip, the homemaker who must hide her coffee when a priesthood leader visits, the business leader who just can't seem to quit smoking, and the teenager who can't stand being left out of the late-night beer bust.

Other people have no trouble with the Word of Wisdom at all, but they simply can't see how they can pay tithing and still make ends meet. Still others may do all this but have absolutely no control over the purity of their thoughts. Others might vocalize endlessly about how badly the Brethren goofed when they put the dingbat down the street in as their bishop, or about how foolish or boring the temple ceremony is, and on and on ad infinitum. Think of any commandment, and you will probably be able to think of someone who is struggling with it.

As we become adults within the Church, then, we have several choices as to what we will do with the rest of our lives. The most obvious and most popular choice seems to be to do nothing at all, but just to continue to live without any particular direction. We illustrate that in Figure 4.

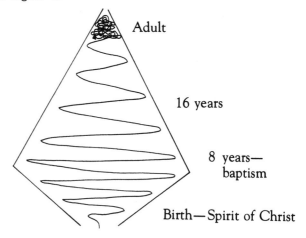

Adult

16 years

8 years— baptism

Birth—Spirit of Christ

Figure 4

Such people spend their entire lives bouncing around within the restrictive upper confines of this triangle, fighting year after year with one or another or perhaps several of the commandments of God. Their main feeling is one of frustration. They see the years passing them by and feel that somehow they are being left behind—and they are fairly accurate in that perception. These people include the returned missionary who suddenly realizes that his zest for the gospel has very nearly disappeared; the mother who finally decides it is easier to skip Relief Society and remain home watching soap operas; the father who decides again and again that as long as he is with his sons there is nothing wrong with a Sunday fishing, hunting or snowmobile excursion; or simply the person who can't get the mattress off his or her back quickly enough to get to meeting. All these good souls are experiencing Mormon frustration for one reason or another. It is slowly eating away at their lives. They just don't have a grip on the commandments yet.

Now what can be done about the Mormon Syndrome? Some people, after a certain amount of time living with this uncomfortable frustration, become discouraged and quit trying. That decision leads to inactivity, apostasy, rebellion. They quit fighting with the commandments by surrendering to their sins. Either gradually or all at once, on purpose or without making any conscious decision, the result is the same. They drop out the bottom of the Church and just go away. (Figure 5.)

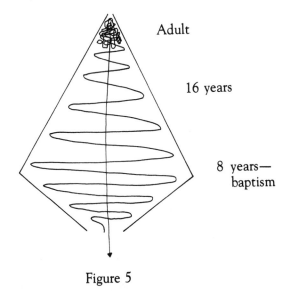

Adult

16 years

8 years—
baptism

Figure 5

Another choice is to pick one or more of God's commandments and rebel against it so forcefully and so violently, banging
with such force against the restrictive sides of the triangle, that the
person ultimately breaks clear through. This is illustrated in Figure
6.

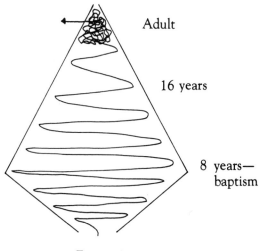

Figure 6

Such people have also left the Church, but they have done so
through overt sin and often Church court procedure. Instead of
sliding away, they went with a splash, spreading pain far and wide.

The Mormon Syndrome—frustration resulting from an unsuc-
cessful struggle to obey the commandments—apparently leads
either to more frustration, to inactivity, or to excommunication.

There is still another possible escape from the frustration of the
Mormon Syndrome. It is not easy and was not intended to be so.
Furthermore, it can only be understood when our concepts of the
commandments of God change. Instead of viewing them as obstruc-
tions to our happiness and handling them in that manner, we must
perceive them as vehicles placed before us to guide us to a particular
destination. We must also realize that they will do so at a more
rapid rate than we might otherwise travel, and will in fact move as
rapidly as we are willing to let them go.

Behold I have given unto you my gospel, and this is the
gospel which I have given unto you—that I came into the world
to do the will of my Father, because my Father sent me.

And my Father sent me that I might be lifted up upon the cross; that I might draw all men unto me, that as I have been lifted up by men even so should men be lifted up by the Father, to stand before me, to be judged of their works, whether they be good or whether they be evil—

And for this cause have I been lifted up; therefore, according to the power of the Father I will draw all men unto me, that they may be judged according to their works.

And it shall come to pass, that whoso repenteth and is baptized in my name shall be filled; and if he endureth to the end, behold, him will I hold guiltless before my Father at that day when I shall stand to judge the world.

And he that endureth not unto the end, the same is he that is also hewn down and cast into the fire, from whence they can no more return, because of the justice of the Father.

And this is the word which he hath given unto the children of men. And for this cause he fulfilleth the words which he hath given, and he lieth not, but fulfilleth all his words.

And no unclean thing can enter into his kingdom; therefore nothing entereth into his rest save it be those who have washed their garments in my blood, because of their faith, and the repentance of all their sins, and their faithfulness unto the end.

Now this is the commandment: Repent, all ye ends of the earth, and come unto me and be baptized in my name, that ye may be sanctified by the reception of the Holy Ghost, that ye may stand spotless before me at the last day.

Verily, verily, I say unto you, this is my gospel; and ye know the things that ye must do in my church; for the works that ye have seen me do that shall ye also do; for that which ye have seen me do even that shall ye do;

Therefore, if ye do these things blessed are ye, for ye shall be lifted up at the last day. (3 Ne. 27:13-22.)

Jesus was sent into the world to die upon the cross, thus gaining power to judge all men and cleanse them of their sins. Of course this is done only if they will repent of them at some point in their lives and then continue from that day in striving to keep the commandments, enduring to the end.

This is the Atonement, and Christ tells us that it is also the gospel, in total.

Commandments, then, are the vehicles which we may ride, if you will, to the feet of the Savior, where he will lift us up and present us to the Father.

Once we have adjusted our attitude toward the commandments and embraced them as blessings rather than hindrances, we will recognize the fourth answer to the Mormon Syndrome.

The fourth direction is up—into a very narrow and restricted area, but up nevertheless. (Figure 7.) How does one move up from that area of frustration? We can't walk, jump, run, or climb: the only way to move up into the neck of the funnel is through prayer and the right attitude. And the key word here is dedication.

Figure 7

To move up into the neck, each person must reach a point where he is willing to get upon his knees, acknowledge Jesus Christ as his Savior, and then formally dedicate his life to him. Christ can have us, when we are so dedicated, for whatever purpose he chooses; he can have anything of ours that he needs, including our own life.

We commit ourselves to the fact that he is Christ; we now trust him and his judgment completely; we will submit to whatever he might ask of us; and we will do so with joy.

> And we know also, that sanctification through the grace of our Lord and Savior Jesus Christ is just and true, to all those who love and serve God with all their mights, minds, and strength. (D&C 20:31.)

There it is, the blessing that comes from dedication: *sanctification.* What does it mean to be sanctified? According to the dictionary, it means "to be made pure and holy."

When we (the authors) came across this scripture and the idea of sanctification, we had never heard it talked about in Church; no one had ever discussed it in any classes we had had; we couldn't recall our parents ever mentioning it; as we searched the scriptures we found passage after passage in the Doctrine and Covenants that stressed it. A few of them:

1. Sanctification is a gift given because of obedience to law. (D&C 88:33-35.)

2. Sanctification comes by magnifying the priesthood. (D&C 84:33.)

3. Sanctification is the reward of our own efforts. (D&C 43:9-11.)

4. Sanctification comes after an individual dedicates his life to the service of Heavenly Father. It then becomes available through the grace or goodness (the gift) of Jesus Christ. (D&C 20:31.)

5. A person cannot become sanctified until he has literally proven himself worthy of it, through severe trials and tests. (D&C 101:4-5.)

6. The sanctified will have the opportunity of seeing God, when he chooses to reveal himself to them. (D&C 88:68.)

7. Only the sanctified are of the celestial world. (D&C 88:2.)

8. The sanctified are continually in the presence of God after this life. (D&C 76:21.)

And that is just a sample from *one* of the standard works!

When we dedicate our lives, we are ready to enter into the narrow passage which represents our testing period. We have just made a commitment to Heavenly Father, and in effect he looks down upon us and says, "Very well, we will test you now, as we did Abraham, to show you whether or not you are sincere in your promise of dedication."

This testing, explained in D&C 101:4-5, will be geared for each one of us on an individual basis, will be based on God's intimate understanding of our own strengths and weaknesses, and is another reason why we experience some of the storms of life. The testing may last for weeks, months, or even years, depending upon our needs, but when we are finally able to state absolutely that we are bound to serve God no matter what the costs, then we suddenly emerge from the neck of the funnel and enter into a remarkable experience. (Figure 8.)

Once people enter into this area of life, many remarkable things occur. Their vision of life is suddenly broadened with understanding given by the Holy Ghost. They look upon sin only with abhorrence, meaning that the temporal commandments so many of us struggle with are now second nature to them and they live them

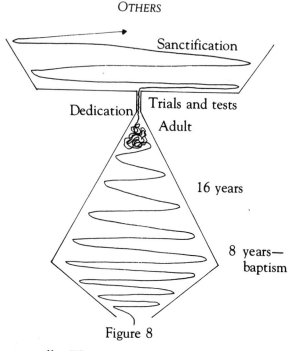

Figure 8

almost automatically. They no longer worry about themselves and can now spend their time in the service of others, thus fulfilling their promise to serve God. (Mos. 2:17.)

And, most significantly, their climb upward while in mortality is only beginning, for the scriptures teach us of many, many blessings that follow sanctification.

This is the beginning of an understanding of the magnificent gift of caring that Christ has given us, called the plan of salvation. This program, begun in mortality, must be totally completed before any of us will gain exaltation in the celestial kingdom. Only the sanctified, those who are pure and holy, will dwell in the presence of God.

But the exciting thing is that now we finally understand our potential, now we comprehend the possibilities that lie before us. Through the perfect love, the perfect caring, of our elder brother Jesus Christ, any and all of us can do it.

> For Christ also hath once suffered for sins, the just for the unjust, that he might bring us to God, being put to death in the flesh, but quickened by the Spirit. (1 Pet. 3:18.)

We are all unjust, we have all sinned, we are all unclean; but if we will only repent of our sins the atonement of Christ will make us spotless so that we will stand justified before God at the last day.

But now, suppose that we know all this, but somehow it just isn't important enough to bring about that mighty change called repentance. What happens then?

> Therefore I command you to repent—repent, lest I smite you by the rod of my mouth, and by my wrath, and by my anger, and your sufferings be sore—how sore you know not, how exquisite you know not, yea, how hard to bear you know not.
>
> For behold, I, God, have suffered these things for all, that they might not suffer if they would repent;
>
> But if they would not repent they must suffer even as I;
>
> Which suffering caused myself, even God, the greatest of all, to tremble because of pain, and to bleed at every pore, and to suffer both body and spirit—and would that I might not drink the bitter cup, and shrink—
>
> Nevertheless, glory be to the Father, and I partook and finished my preparations unto the children of men. (D&C 19:15-19.)

If we choose to avoid or reject repentance and refuse to live the commandments, including caring for others, then we must suffer even as he, yet not unselfishly, to free others from their sins, but miserably to pay the price of our own selfishness.

To provide us with as great an opportunity as possible to partake of the blessings of repentance and thus of the Atonement, we have all been given another gift, the Holy Ghost. We received this gift at our confirmation, and we have all had experiences since then that let us know that the gift is, at least occasionally, in effect.

Yet we are told that we cannot become sanctified or made pure and holy without the constant influence of the Holy Ghost in our lives. So how do we keep the Holy Ghost with us constantly? Again Heavenly Father has been kind enough to give us the answer, and in doing so he not only tells us how to keep the Holy Ghost with us at all times, but he also tells us what other major blessings will be ours if and when we do:

> Let thy bowels also be full of charity towards all men, and to the household of faith, and let virtue garnish thy thoughts unceasingly; then shall thy confidence wax strong in the presence of God; and the doctrine of the priesthood shall distil upon thy soul as the dews from heaven.
>
> *The Holy Ghost shall be thy constant companion*, and thy scepter an unchanging scepter of righteousness and truth; and thy dominion shall be an everlasting dominion, and without compulsory means it shall flow unto thee forever and ever. (D&C 121:45-46; emphasis added.)

Two things we must do if we would have the Holy Ghost as a constant companion. We must fill our whole beings with the pure love of Christ toward all other people, including Church members, and we must keep our minds full of virtuous thoughts and feelings at all times. These are the requirements, and as Paul said, if these are met, so will all the others be met. Love fulfills the law.

There are many promises in the above scripture, promises that will begin fulfillment as quickly as we are ready—promises that will culminate in our exaltation. But the promise that we wish to emphasize here is the promise to have the Holy Ghost with you at all times, guiding and directing you toward the point where you will be made pure and holy through the blood of Christ. The key is first to be worthy of his spiritual presence and second be willing and able to listen when he prompts us. Some examples:

A friend of ours was driving home late one night with his family from a Church assignment. The road was mostly deserted, but as he drove to the bottom of a two-lane overpass the Spirit whispered to him that he should pull over. Having learned during his lifetime to be obedient to such promptings, he immediately did so. Less than a minute later a car came over the top of the overpass traveling at an excessive speed and weaving back and forth over both lanes. It sped past his automobile, missing it by just inches, and continued on down the highway. His life and the lives of his family were spared because he was able and willing to listen.

A woman, whose husband was away from home on business, was awakened one night feeling that she should get her little children outside and call the fire department. She led her children outside, wrapped them with blankets, and then went back in and phoned the fire department and reported a fire, though there was no sign of one in her home. Two or three minutes later, just as the fire truck was coming around the corner, there was an explosion and her home was engulfed in flames. She, too, had been willing and able to listen to the feelings of the Spirit.

A young couple were in their sixth month of having a tiny baby in their home, and they were so thrilled to have a daughter like her. Late one night the wife shook her husband awake to tell him urgently that their little daughter was very sick, and that she had a temperature of over 106 degrees. Without a word her husband arose, dressed, and went in and knelt by his daughter's little crib.

Holding his wife's hand he prayed and asked that his course of action be dictated by the Spirit. He then arose and confidently placed his hands on his tiny daughter's head and blessed her, and when he finished her little body immediately cooled to 98.6 degrees. He had been able and willing to listen.

All of us have the right to be filled with joy and happiness in this life. It is not meant to be a morbid, sad experience. Of course, we cannot receive *total* joy until our souls are reunited in the resurrection (D&C 93:33; 101:36), but keeping the commandments, following the promptings of the Spirit, and serving others will bring us happiness while we are here. There will be sorrows here, yes, but even these will ultimately be turned to joy if we are obedient and endure to the end as we are asked to do.

66 "As I reached the age of fourteen, a love for my youngest sister had really grown strong. I loved her more than I could say, and realized how willing I was to do anything for her.

"When she was only two our family toured England. There was one experience we had that stands out in my mind even today. We were walking in a beautiful park along a river. I was on my own and the rest of my family and my relatives were farther ahead. No one realized that my little sister was missing from the group.

"I clearly remember being physically turned around by some power other than myself so I was facing in the opposite direction. There I watched, paralyzed with fear, as my little sister fell into the river.

"I was a little over a hundred yards from her, but I was in that river and by her side in no more than ten or twelve seconds. Keeping her head out of the water I brought her back to the side of the river. By this time I was totally exhausted, and I knew it would be foolish for me to attempt to carry her up the riverbank. Glancing up, I saw the others racing towards us, and I could hear my little sister's heavy and rather uneven breathing.

"I offered a word of thanks to the Lord for granting me the strength and ability necessary to save her from drowning, and for turning me around so I could see her fall into the river." **99**

Caring is vital; there must be no doubt of this. If we are being obedient to the commandments of an all-wise Heavenly Father, then we must care for ourselves, care for our families and loved ones, and, finally, care for all mankind. In this way we have been promised happiness here and life eternal hereafter. To help us learn to do this, we have been given the unconditional love of Heavenly Father, which we must use as an example in our caring. Because we are his children he loves every one of us with infinite kindness, infinite patience, and infinite understanding. Once we realize that and accept it as fact, we are on our way.

Two very good friends, Sister Phyllis Inouye and Brother Don H. Smith, have shared with us two very special experiences which we would like to share with you in closing. These two accounts beautifully illustrate the kind of love our Heavenly Father has for us, his literal children. As you read these, and as you go forth to care, we pray that our Heavenly Father will bless and be with you and give you an understanding of the goodness and greatness and importance of what you are doing. It is his work.

66 "Today I entered the temple, the house of the Lord, to do the work that he expects of me. During this particular session an experience occurred that I shall never forget. I have always had a testimony concerning the great love that our Father in heaven has for his children—the unconditional love that he has for me. Today his love was made known to me in a way I have never experienced before.

"The session was like others that I have had the privilege of attending, but near the end something was different. A temple worker took my hand, and as we touched I felt an intense warmth radiate from his hand into my body. He was large in stature and spoke with a very slow but sure speech. I began to feel as though I were melting down to a miniature me, and a feeling of great love completely engulfed me. I felt total peace and humility.

"I don't remember speaking to this man, but I do remember that all I did was slow and sure, not like some of my other experiences there. As I passed him I looked up at him and found him to be younger than most of the other workers. He looked down at me also, and smiled.

"As I now ponder this experience in my mind and pray about it, I understand that this is a taste of how I will feel in the presence of my Father in heaven. His unfeigned love will radiate through my being, giving to me complete happiness and total peace of mind.

"I know without any doubt that the Holy Ghost made known God's love to me today, God's total love. With this knowledge I know that I can perform in this life any task he might ask of me, and endure any trial he might ask me to endure." **99**

66 "Suzie, our youngest child, was born with cerebral palsy, and has never walked a step in her life. So we had to have someone take care of her day and night. Our little boy Cory took over that assignment, day and night, for years.

"When Cory was about nine we went to a ward Decoration Day picnic. When we got there Cory wandered over to where a man had several boxes of turtles and toads for sale. In a few minutes Cory came running back shouting, 'Daddy, Daddy, can I buy a horny toad?' Our boy had never seen any of those things, and he was very excited. He had one in his hand and he wanted to buy it.

"I asked him how much it was, and he told me thirty-five cents. I am the last of the big spenders, so I said, 'Sure, Son. Does the man have two?' He said yes, so I suggested that he buy one for Tommy, who lived across the street, and I gave him a dollar.

"He came back proudly holding two toads. He took one over to Tommy, and over the next few weeks they played with them together, and they grew quite fond of them. So now he could watch little Suzie and play with his horny toad at the same time, and when we put him to bed at night we'd have to go in after he was asleep and take his little toad out of his hand, he loved it so much.

"After Cory had it about two months, he and Tommy were playing out on the front lawn and Tommy's toad got away. It got under the house, and they couldn't find it. They were terribly upset about it. They looked for it for days, but they never did find it. So Cory got even closer to his toad.

"About two months later Tommy came over and Cory hadn't come home from school yet. Tommy asked, 'Mrs. Smith, can I play with Cory's toad, please?' She said he could and told him to go ahead. He took it out and was playing with it in the back yard when his mother called him to come home. So Tommy just set the horny toad on the end of the diving board and ran home. Cory and I got home together about two hours later, and a few minutes later he let out this blood-curdling scream, and I ran out the back door to see what was wrong. He was standing on his toes, right on the edge of the pool, looking down at the toad which was stretched out on the drain. It had been there for two hours, and of course it was dead, and he just sobbed, 'Daddy, Daddy, what can I do?'

"Cory's ears were under treatment at that time, and so he couldn't dive down and get it out. I wasn't really fond of the toad myself, and so I wasn't about to dive down to get it. But Cory cried and cried.

"About that time his older brother, Terry, came out and said, 'I'm not going to touch that toad, it's dead!' But we convinced him that if it was dead, it really wouldn't hurt him if he would dive down and get it.

"We got an egg carton and cut two inches off the end of it, and Terry dived down and brought the toad back up to Cory. I was standing at the edge of the pool when Terry brought the dead toad up and handed it to Cory, who just sobbed and sobbed as he held it in his hand. In desperation, Cory sobbed, 'Daddy, Daddy, what shall I do?'

"Well, it about broke my heart, and so very sympathetically I said, 'Why don't you just throw it in the trash?'

"With that, he just cried all the harder, and so I said, 'Son, I'm sorry, I'm sorry! There's nothing you can do for that toad now. It's been dead for over two hours. Why don't you just put it on the fireplace over there, and tomorrow morning you and I will go out and bury it.'

"I started to walk away. Terry, who was a deacon then, was lying on the edge of the diving board, and he said, 'Dad?' I asked him what he wanted, and he didn't say anything, so I started to walk on. Again Terry said, 'Dad?' Again I asked him what he wanted, and again he didn't answer. So I was just ready to go through the door when he said, 'Dad?' I said, 'Terry, *what do you want?*' And he said, 'I was just wondering if you could give that toad a blessing.'

"I said, 'Son, you can't give that little toad a blessing. It has been dead for two and a half hours.' He said, 'But Dad, when I was so sick at Christmas and the doctor couldn't help, you gave me a blessing and I got better right away. So I don't see why you can't give Cory's toad a blessing.'

"I said, 'Because it's just a toad!' and went into the house. But then I asked myself, was it just a toad? Not to Cory, it wasn't. That little toad was one of the priceless things of his life. So he and Terry took it into the bathroom, and I didn't hear this prayer, but I know that this is the gist of it. Cory got down on his knees, and he said, 'Dear Heavenly Father, please bless my little sister. Bless her that people will be kind to her, and that she will be able to have fun with other little kids. And please give me back my little toad.'

"He then took the toad out and put it on the fireplace. About nine that night I told Cory to go to bed, so he went out and pushed his toad, and it was as stiff as a board. Dead. So he went up to his room and got on his knees again and said, 'Dear God, please bless my little sister. Bless her that people will be good to her so she can have fun, and please give me back my little toad.'

"The next morning was Saturday, and we were all sleeping in, and Cory got up about seven o'clock and went out to his little toad that had now been dead for sixteen hours. It was still stiff and dead and withered up, so he picked it up and came back to his bedroom and got on his knees again. And he didn't just pray. This little boy literally talked to God.

" 'Please Heavenly Father, please bless my little sister, help her to have fun, and bless her that people will be kind to her so she can do the things that other little kids can do. And please give me back my little toad.'

"Then he came out of his bedroom and took hold of me and said, 'Daddy, Daddy, look Daddy. My little toad was just asleep. See his eyes, he's awake now.'

"That little toad was alive! Now I ask, who are we? Who are we? Does God love us? He does, and he blesses us according to our obedience, no matter how old we are or how unimportant what we are asking for may seem to others. I know!" **"**

INDEX

Book designed by Two's Company
Composed by Type Design
in Goudy Book
Printed by Publishers Press
on Bookcraft Antique
Bound by Mountain States Bindery
in Sturdetan, Gunmetal, Skivar